AF541159

THE HEART-BRAIN RELATIONSHIP

THE HEART-BRAIN RELATIONSHIP

By

K.S.V. Phanindra

B.Tech

MVGR College of Engineering

Vizianagaram Andhra Pradesh

(INDIA)

DISCOVERY PUBLISHING HOUSE PVT. LTD.

NEW DELHI-110 002

Published by:

Tilak Wasan

DISCOVERY PUBLISHING HOUSE PVT. LTD.
4383/4B, Ansari Road, Darya Ganj
New Delhi-110 002 (India)
Phone : +91-11-23279245, 43596064-65
Fax : +91-11-23253475
E-mail : discoverypublishinghouse@gmail.com
sales@discoverypublishinggroup.com
parul.wasan@gmail.com
web : www.discoverypublishinggroup.com

***First Edition:* 2014**

ISBN: 978-93-5056-438-7

The Heart-Brain Relationship

Printed at:
Dynamic Printers
Delhi

This Book is Dedicated to Me
The Amalgam of All The People in
My Life and Me

Preface

Hello readers! 'The Heart-Brain Relationship' is not just a book for me. It is my dream. This is a path by which I gave form to my interest in psychology. During my first year of under-graduation I was thinking how to work on psychology by balancing it with my regular studies and this is the thought I got – write a book and use it as a path for self-development and to quench my thirst of psychology. I worked on it for more than three years and this is the result of it. I framed theories on various things. I worked on self-developed techniques and developed many theories to explain the mental structure and techniques for self-development. I am happy to say that all the theories and techniques in this book are thoroughly developed using logic, analysis, survey and intuition.

In the book 'Letters to Thinkers', Edward De Bono quoted 'ignorance allowed me to do mine just in a different way' while explaining that things can be viewed differently and new basic concepts can be created better by working on things without learning the existing methods. I did the same and as a result, developed a theory of mental structure which is very much similar to that which ancient Greeks portrayed and the recent researches in neuroscience had confirmed. In this book, I developed new ways of looking things. I don't say these ways are the right ways and the others are wrong as I don't believe in existence of right or wrong ways. They are not completely right or completely wrong but are just ways with some having more positive and some having more negative qualities. I also believe in relativity of techniques. A theory which applies to me may or may not apply to you, that is, no theory is completely universal in nature. So, in most cases, I just put forward the characteristics of the theories and techniques. You have to mould them in the way they suit you.

To build a better us effectively, we have to understand and mould our inner self. For this our mental structure is to be understood well. In the theory proposed by me, the heart and brain are taken as two different and interacting fundamental blocks of our mental structure. *'The latest research in neuroscience confirms that emotion and cognition can best be thought of as separate but interacting functions or systems, each with its unique intelligence'*. The means of controlling them individually and the means of controlling their relationship are explained in detail. In this book, first the introduction to 'The Heart-Brain Relationship' is explained discussing the characteristics of the heart, the brain and their relationship. Then the strengths and the weaknesses of a student and his relationship with the educational system are discussed. As it is important to know the various factors which affect us, the influence of the parents, friends, and society on us is also discussed. The techniques involved in setting a proper heart-brain relationship are analysed. These include the tools of logical thinking, controlling the mind, converting negatives into positives, and self-analysis. The ideas of an ideal student and an ideal education system are put forward. The last chapter 'The Framework of Mind' discusses the integrated mental system combining all the aspects.

I am a child transforming into an adult attaining maturity. I am a student at the edge of formal education completely aware of the system and life of a student and child. I am a person passionate about psychology, a stream completely different to my education, and working in the 'art for the art's sake' way in a completely different dimension. I have been teaching students for about five years and have played an important role in mentoring them to attain their higher goals. I have been counselling many people to help them overcome their psychological problems. This book is about the children, students, adults, system, and self. I am a conglomeration of all these making me a uniquely suitable for writing this book.

Don't just read this book! Understand it completely. Apply the techniques in this book as you read. It gives you as much as you want and as much you extract.

— **Author**

Acknowledgements

This book would have been incomplete without the assistance of all those who have helped and encouraged me. I thank all of them for all their support.

K.S.V. Phanindra

Contents

1.	Introduction	1
2.	The Heart-Brain Relationship *The Base*	4
3.	Students and Educational System *A Teacher or a Troubler?*	12
4.	Students' Strengths *Fortify the Power*	19
5.	Parents *The First Teachers*	26
6.	Friends and Society *The Guide*	34
7.	Logical Thinking *The Essence*	38
8.	Controlling the Mind *Tame the Shire*	42
9.	Converting Negatives into Positives *The Change*	51
10.	Self-analysis *Reveal the Secrets*	54
11.	Ideal Student *The Vision*	57

12. **Ideal Educational System** *Unattainable?* — 60

13. **The Framework of Mind** *The Inner Us* — 64

14. **Understanding Ourselves** *Do I Know Me?* — 71

15. **Live Your Life** *Your Way* — 76

16. **A Word by the Author** — 79

17. **Quotes** *A Source of Inspiration* — 80

Index — 85

1 Introduction

> The beauty of an action lies in the process of doing it.
>
> **— K.S.V. Phanindra**

Do you have dreams? Are they forgotten as crazy speculations or did you transform them into passionate goals? Did you try to achieve your passionate goals by transforming them into strategic actions or did you let the society and time suppress them?

I have dreams evolved from diversified interests which I transformed into passionate goals and then into strategic actions. Psychology is one of my passions and this book is the result of my strategic actions in that direction.

I started working on cognitive, child and educational psychology. I developed a set of theories which accurately explain our mental framework and effective techniques which helps us in self development and presented most of them in this book.

When I was doing the final draft of this book, I found out that the structure of the mental framework proposed by me was not invented but had been reinvented by me. This method of treating the heart and brain as two different elements of our mental framework which interact with each other was first thought of by ancient Greeks. And 'www.heartboard.com' supports this quoting:

'The latest research in neuroscience confirms that emotion and cognition can best be thought of as separate but interacting functions or systems, each with its unique intelligence'.

At any point of time, we experience two things — thoughts and feelings. Though both occur in brain, feelings are accompanied by various physiological changes. For example, anger is the rapid generation of energy in the muscles. Feelings are traditionally said to originate from heart. We can treat heart and brain as two different elements which interact between themselves and with external factors and act upon us together. This is the base of the mental framework proposed by me.

This book deals with consciously building a better mental framework and changing ourselves from the roots. The best way to analyse or deal with any situation is by employing the cause-effect-remedy method. We have to first find the cause of the situation, find how it affects us and then develop a strategy to deal with the situation. In this case, we have to understand the basic blocks of our mental framework—the brain and the heart. We should have a clear idea of their characteristics and the relation between them to analyse whole of the mental framework.

After analysing the structure of the framework we have to understand the various factors which influence us. The factors which influence us are part of the environment around us. This includes parents, friends, educational system, society, and all the people and situations we encounter in life. Analysing them helps us in understanding the influences on us and in controlling them.

The important part in this process of building a better us is to control the affects of the external factors on us. Having already analysed the way they affect us, we can regulate their affects. This helps us to be the way we want. For this we have to learn various self-development processes and tools. The basic tool and the greatest strength of humans is the logical thinking. We have to learn to control our mind and rectify our negatives using this tool. However we have to first identify our mistakes. Self-analysis comes into play here.

This book lucubrates this process and gives a clear insight into it. This book is just a guide. It explains the nature of the things and the ways to deal with them. You should put it to work.

2

The Heart-Brain Relationship

The Base

This is my simple religion. There is no need for temples; no need for complicated philosophy. Our own brain, our own heart is our temple; the philosophy is kindness.

— Dalai Lama

The brain gives the heart its sight. The heart gives the brain its vision.

— Kall

There is a world in us, the world of the Heart and the Brain – the two building blocks of us. The external world we live in is an image of this internal world. The Heart and the Brain – the true governors of us – act separately and in combination to control us.

The heart and the brain being the controlling elements, affect all our decisions and the way we approach things. So, our complete understanding of them is very important. Understanding each of the heart and the brain is individually complex and the combination of them is far more complex and delicate. So for understanding them better we have to first understand each of them individually and then the delicate relation between them.

The heart and the brain are two different entities. We normally treat them as a single entity as we see only the effect caused by the heart-brain relationship. Both can create or destroy our system if we do not control them properly.

Normally we don't go to the inner us and build a system to control us, but, we do have an inbuilt control system in our sub-conscious mind. But to make it more efficient and to build a better us, we need to build it consciously.

The Heart

Feelings! That is what the heart is made up of. It may be one word but that one word makes us human.

Heart is an extremely sensitive element. Each and every incident and thought affects the heart and every thought and action is in turn affected by it. Heart determines our attitude towards people and situations. It determines our opinion and hence our reactions towards them. While the brain runs the thoughts, heart turns them. Heart has such great power. Heart creates problems by interfering with the thought process. This causes deviation from the path of logic.

One of the distorting factors of the heart is an unwanted and overweighed feeling. This disturbs our thought process. Feelings are extremely important to us. But if they are overweighed or negatively shaded, they simply distort the thought process and consequently distort the individual. At times, they can even drive us to extremities like depression, frustration, anger and so on. These unwanted feelings couple up with imaginations and distorts us. Maintaining the feelings and not letting them go to the threshold limits is called emotional balance. Proper emotional balance helps us to work properly at all times.

Another important factor of the heart is fear. Fear is mainly triggered by imagination. Fear multiplies the negative effects making the positive ones look small. It moves us into a virtual state where we fear even the unnecessary and small things. It hinders us from making decisions and moving forward. This does not allow us to take the risky path which may be a better path or the path we are interested in. Another problem with fear is, it restricts our positive thinking and changes our thought process. It even has the power to completely take the control over the brain and its thought process making us its prisoner. It does not allow free flow of thoughts. Fear also builds up stress on us. The cumulative property of fear-imagination pair makes it worse. When a small fear is build up, imagination makes it grow. This fear can be nullified by controlling negative imagination and thought process and by fighting fear at the right time. Any delay accumulates fear in us. As Franklin D.Roosevelt said: 'The only thing we have to fear is fear itself'.

Blind faith is another negative influence peddler of our system. We confuse between pure and impure faith. Pure faith is a result of perfect heart-brain relationship in the innermost parts of our heart and brain. Blind faith is a surfaced one which is affected by the external factors and depends on the situation. It being affected by external factors shifts us away from neutral thinking. It can be said in a more simple way that it biases our thinking. For example, if we believe that someone is bad or something is bad, framed from the third party inputs, our attitude towards them will be so. We judge them to be wrong for unknown reason even if they are good. That means blind faith biases our judgment and decisions. The same principle explains the case of superstitions. People understand religion and culture in a wrong way. They give more priority to idols and God but not to the principles of the religion. Similarly, we think we are in the right path without analysing our thoughts and actions. We believe in many things without proper reason. Blind faith may put us in the wrong path as we are no longer in the path of logic. We will not be flexible to the surroundings. For example, a person was in a wrong path and by realizing his mistakes, is trying to change, instead of encouraging him;

we suppress him by treating him the old way. This prevents him from changing. This may even lead the person to great depression. This is the case with many people who are trying to change. Whenever we try to change, the society tends to oppose that change. Only those who find a proper way succeed in changing into a new better person. Most of the others end up becoming worse or going into depression. We can differentiate between the pure faith and the blind faith using logic and ethics.

The Brain

Even though heart is the main distorting element of the brain, brain has a few irregularities and some factors which tend to cause irregularities.

Brain's extreme sensitivity is the main cause of its deviations. It gets easily affected by even small factors and tends to deviate. This sensitivity is to be tackled carefully and the deviations are to be controlled. Brain can be sensitive in both positive and negative direction. This sensitivity can be used to our aid by orienting the brain in the positive direction.

Brain is highly vulnerable to heart. This causes deviation of the brain from the path of logic. The affect of the heart on the brain is to be filtered and only the positive affects are to be passed over to the inner part of the brain where the sub-conscious control of us is done.

An isolated brain is highly stable and orderly. This feature makes humans superior to other species. Brain's greatest power is to think by logic. Techniques to apply this tool are to be developed and applied. We have to nurture the ability to use logic and dissolve it deep in us.

Apart from logic, brain also has a huge amount of energy bound in it. This energy powers up the brain. We use a part of it in the activities of our brain and some more of it is consumed subconsciously by the brain. The total amount used by us is still just a small part of what our brain possesses. We have to release the remaining energy and utilise it.

To utilise the complete power of brain, we have to control the thought process of the brain. We have to make it stronger, well-structured and powerful. During the process of building it, we should even embed modules into the process which take care of handling the effects of the heart, the external factors and the disturbances. Once we build a good thought process, it takes care of the whole of controlling us.

The Relationship

Even though heart and brain are the two things which govern us, they don't act individually. They always act together, however in different proportions based on the context. It is the heart-brain relationship which has its direct effect on us. Maintaining the heart-brain relationship in the right proportion keeps our brain in proper order. Everything from the decisions we make to the internal thought process depends on the status of the relationship at that point of time. The aim of all the techniques we apply to keep our brain in the right order is to maintain the heart-brain relationship in the most optimal proportion. But what is optimal proportion of the heart and the brain in the heart-brain relationship? The optimal proportion refers to the ratio of the contribution of the heart and the brain to the relationship which helps us to be in the stable state. It creates a positive environment within us and sets the heart and the brain in synchronous with each other.

This heart-brain relationship is complex as it combines the two complex and sensitive elements which are very much different from each other but still are as much similar. The high sensitivity and cumulative natures of the heart and the brain don't just make them individually complex but also makes their relation far more complex. The heart and brain has another property of aiding each other. These properties are to be clearly understood along with the individual factors of the heart and the brain to understand their relationship.

The cumulative nature of the heart, the brain and of their relationship causes rapid movement of thoughts in a single path taking only the supporting factors into consideration which may be positive or negative. This accumulation of thoughts and/or feelings can drive the relationship towards instability. A thought introduced by the brain gets affected by a feeling of the heart. This feeling may be in the line of the thought or opposite to it. The immense power of the heart may mislead the thought process of a weakly controlled brain. The heart normally creates turbulence in the brain which may lead to confusion and negative thinking. The cause of this may be a possible hindrance or a problem we are likely to face in the future. This in turn serves as an input to the heart and may lead to either of the extremes – fear, depression, anxiety or a highly excited state. These build up a huge amount of stress on the brain, thereby driving both the brain and the heart towards extremities and causes instability. In the extreme states, both the heart and the brain will be either entirely dull and numb or over-excited. These states are the states unsuitable for thinking which, at the moment may be a necessity for tackling the situation. The only way to keep it in control is by balancing the heart and the brain in the right proportion.

One of the worst properties of an uncontrolled heart-brain relationship is it causes the tendency of the heart and the brain to move more rapidly towards the negatives. Sometimes, we can find ourselves encouraging negative thoughts and feelings. Why is it so? This tendency is due to some of the basic factors like the fear of the heart and the vulnerability of the brain. Fear covers up our real self. It couples up with an out-of-order brain and drives us out of logic and develops negative thoughts. Fear also creates a mask over the problem making it looking huge and tough. Fear even has the ability to numb our brain. The fear can be eliminated by filtering it with logic and a good thought process. This breaks up the negative fear and only takes in the actual problem.

An uncontrolled heart-brain relationship even biases our thought process. When the heart-brain relationship is not in right proportion, then one of them may be more than the optimal proportion and the other may be less. Due to this, the thought process may be biased. Let us say the heart is more than the right proportion in one of the situations. The feeling of the heart has the property to distort thought. Heart fills us with false opinions and fear shifting us away from the neutral thought. The biasing may be observed not just due to the opinions formed due to the external sources but may also be due to the first impressions, negative quality of the person to which we are not in the least linked with, and our mood or the state of our heart-brain relationship.

Generally, our first impression affects our thought process a lot. That is the reason why it is said that the first impressions are the best impressions. But it is a wrong approach as any person and many situations are too complex to be judged at the first instant. So, it often misleads us. If our first impression on a person is negative, it normally fixes our opinion on the person and treats him in that way even if we are not dealing with the part of the person which has the negative quality. This causes biasing of our thoughts. The same is even applicable to situations and other entities. For example, if we feel a particular subject is difficult just because we didn't understand the first topic, we will possibly fear the subject and thus will not be reading it interestingly.

Another biasing factor of our thought is the basis of our judgment of a person or a situation. Every person has both positive and negative qualities. A person with a negative quality is normally judged to be bad. But a small mark on a white sheet doesn't make it dirty and useless. The paper still remains much clean and usable. Another problem is we don't concentrate on the right point. We have to concentrate exactly on the quality of a person which is linked with the point we are dealing with. We have to accept the people along with their positive and negative qualities.

Our instantaneous state of the heart-brain relationship or mood is another important biasing factor. While the other factors are almost fixed, this is a continuously varying factor. Our sensitivity and varying external influences are the prime reasons for this. Our mood at a particular instant determines our attitude and orientation of tackling the situation. So it is important to control our mood.

It can be observed that the biasing factors are mostly external factors. But their affect on us is through the internal factors. The reason for this is our inability to limit, filter and differentiate the external factors. The external factors are strong, uncontrollable, and continuously changing. But we are stronger than them and have the ability to manage them. All we need to do is to find a path to do it. Even though the external factors are strong, they are entirely powerless without the aid of the internal factors. The influence of the external factors can be governed by controlling the internal factors.

3

Students and Educational System

A Teacher or a Troubler?

The only thing that interferes with my learning is my education.

— Albert Einstein

I've never let my school interfere with my education.

— Mark Twain

Present Educational System

Every system has both positives and negatives. We normally refer to only one of them considering the one which has greater magnitude. This approach biases our analysis. So here, I try to discuss the positives and the negatives of the present educational system and then their effect on the students' thinking and behaviour.

The present educational system has evolved as a result of many changes over thousands of years. The process of change is perennial. But what matters is whether it is taking a positive or a negative turn. This system being highly dynamic in nature is difficult to analyse. So I discuss a few points discretely.

When a student gets fed up with all the hard work he is doing and can't find the reason to do it, he just tries to move to a lower stress level. It is in accordance with the fundamental law of the nature – every substance in the world tries to move from higher energy level to the lower energy level. Higher stress means the brain is in excited or loaded state. So it tries to come to the lower level energy state. What happens when a small breach appears on the wall of a pipe? The water oozes out. This tears the wall of the pipe. Similarly the high pressure on the student tends to disturb his mental framework.

Stress is not the only problem of the present educational system. The mode of teaching awaits a change. The topics or concepts are not explained in the way which helps the students to build new concepts. In the present system, a theory is directly discussed without giving importance to its evolution. A better way of explaining a topic is to first create the conditions actually present at the time that concept was developed, discuss evolution of the theory and then discuss the theory. The principle advantage of the second way to that of the first is, the student will be able to learn to form a logic map to overcome the problems and they will be able to develop new theories in future. Whereas, in the first way, the method is similar to reverse engineering and the student will only be able to deduce the reason of using a particular component in a system. The second method is even to be implemented in the books to the extent possible.

Another important negative of the present system is the ineffectiveness its system of evaluating a student. Surely there is a great need to differentiate between students' abilities and knowledge or in my view the ability to use the knowledge in a good and efficient manner. And also, a universal form of measure of these abilities is needed. Here enters the method of marks. It was an effective way. But it is not now! This is due to the acceptance of this method by the society in the negative way. When the aim of the student is to get marks, he can do it in anyway. Most of the students now follow the easier way – to read in the exam point of view. By this the actual essence of introducing marks is faded.

Coming to the positives of our educational system, education makes us socially, psychologically and academically mature. The role of education in our life is more than just qualifying us for a job. The maturity the educational system induces into us is very important and critical too. Education brings people together and makes him ready to challenges in the outer world. Education also acts as a platform for the development of human intelligence. Education also equips us with information and techniques required to sustain the outer world for ourselves.

The role of education in developing maturity can be explained by an example. There are many jobs for which the qualification required is a degree but can be done by a secondary school passed-out with some training. So, what is the need of doing a degree for the job? Education in a patterned and step-by-step way increases the ability in us to analyse, apply, build, and learn. Simply, it improves our intelligence and makes us more psychologically mature. The more we learn the more are these qualities amplified. Education also brings us in touch with problems making us stronger to face more, building confidence in us and giving us required experience.

Effect of Education on Thinking

As the method of reading for marks has rooted in the students' brains, students target marks but not the knowledge. If marks are the criteria, the student can do it in many ways. He works for long hours. He just mugs up the things from the books. As there are millions of students like this, even the society takes advantage. They print books which have ready made information and have very little scope for analysing. Corporate system which helps the students to get the marks without any difficulty is introduced that has attracted a lot of students (even more parents). Now the corporate system had taken lead. This system influenced the students a lot and just makes the students get used to material, low quality work. This in turn creates a lot of stress including stress due to exams, stress by work, stress by parents, and stress due to society on our mind. He has to adjust many things in him in right proportions. He has to work hard to complete the works, to get the marks, to manage the time, and to check his character which at last may even become his lowest priority. All these will not leave an inch of space for the brain to relax neither to think. The lack of proper relaxation in turn makes the brain dull, blunt and unhealthy. All these stresses and works make the brain unstable. A student can be loaded but should not be burdened.

Stability of a brain is very important. Even the nature respects stability. Each and everything in the nature tries to attain stability and undergoes reaction. There is movement in this universe just to attain stability. This stability is attained by cancelling the forces applied and attaining minimizing energy. Our brain also accepts this basic law. So the brain tries to attain stability. But when there are different forces continuously driving our brain away from stability, it can't work with full efficiency. In these conditions, it is not possible to get a completely stable mind. But it is surely possible to minimize the gap.

If we minutely examine the system, it inherently develops our thinking. The hurdles we face, the concepts we learn, the problems we solve are the main reasons for this. So, the education system is one prime reason for the development of our thinking. But, due to the lapses in the system, the pattern of our thinking is not very effective in some cases. We have to frame up ways to rectify this.

Effect of Education System on Students' Behaviour

One of the duties of an educational system is to mould the characters of the students. However, this role of educational system is faded and now in a shoddy state. Along with playing very less part in developing the students' character, a few factors of the present system are even affecting it in a negative way. One of the main factors of these is the stress created by the system.

Generally work and competition over a limit leads to stress. That limit is set by the mental framework of the student. In case of a student, high competition and high expectancies from the parents and society are also the causes of stress. It is only in some cases that trying situations causes the stress. The principal component of stress on a student is the educational stress.

The origin of stress is generally an external factor. However, the external factor is just a triggering element. The roots of stress are not the external factors. They are the internal factors. The effect of stress on the brain is similar to the effect caused by other emotions and feelings on the brain – it can keep the brain in order and also distort it. It is due to these reasons that stress can be considered as a feeling in us to analyse its effect on us. Sometimes, under the same pressure, some people (students in this context) appear to be more stressed than the others. This is due to our feeling that we are being stressed. Those who don't feel so appear to be less stressed than those who feel so. This supports our method of taking stress as a feeling.

Considering the educational stress on the student, most students choose the path of material hard work for improving their academic percentages. This may also be due his perception that it is the only way. The present system is encouraging material hard work in which he will be completely taking in data. This makes him to think less as his mind is completely busy taking in the stuff. When the mind is completely in the state of input, it will surely not get a chance to process it. Due to this the brain will not be having any time to relax. So the brain tries to find some means of relaxation through fun. When the brain doesn't get it, then similar to a bomb which is a sudden release of energy, the brain will find ways to relax and have so-called fun with sudden release of energy that may distort the student's stableness. As a result, the child loses control over his behaviour. This can also be explained in an almost similar way with a small difference. Well, when a student gets fed up with all the work he is doing or had done, just as all the substances in the universe move from higher energy level to lower energy level, his brain tries to move out of stress into a lower energy level. Thus whenever the student gets some small gap, just as the gas oozes out of the tightly packed balloon, the student tries to enjoy a lot. And most of the students just can't come back to his regular state thus causing a long term deflection. At some point of time, he may completely lose control over himself. This leads to his character going into the negative zone. While this method is in long term, coming to the effect of stress at a point of time, stress disrupts the brain and makes it numb. For example we can understand concepts better in normal days than just before the exams when the stress is at its peak. Can you run carrying a heavy load on your back? The same thing happens with the brain. Stress loads the brain making it weak and hinders it from working efficiently. Due to this, our effective capability in tackling the particular situation, like understanding the concept and working well for exams in above example, is lowered than our original capability.

I will explain this effect of educational system in an illustrative manner taking the case of heart attack. The whole process of heart attack starts when some small foreign material gets stuck in one of the arteries covering a part of the artery. This causes some restriction to the flow of blood. But as the blood has to fill the requirement, the heart has to use more energy and the blood flows faster. Due to contraction, blood at the contraction flows still faster. This creates a low pressure at that point and the vein contracts still more. This again results in the same process. And cumulatively, the work of the heart increases more and more. This increased contraction and the pressure on the heart causes a lot of strain on the heart and leads to heart attack. Similarly, due to stress our effective capability decreases which results in decreased output. This discourages us and eventually imposes more stress on us. And the cycle repeats. If we do not treat the situation properly in the starting itself, it imposes more and more stress on us.

However there is more than one way educational system influences the student. There are some more students who are affected in a completely different way than the previous one. When the student is burdened heavily with stress, he gets suppressed still more and becomes a very dull and depressed fellow. He may be so depressed that he even can't talk freely with his parents. He may be a book worm but will not be developed in any way. Even his feelings get suppressed. It is mainly the role of parents to identify such children and find their actual problem and solve it.

Coming to the positive part of the stress, stress helps us to keep us working. Without stress, we may not be working continuously. However, the stress should not be a burden for us. So, stress in its limits keeps us working by creating a reason to work.

The negative effect of stress can be greatly filtered by applying 'the art of differentiation' discussed later. The heart plays more role than the brain in creating stress. Stress is mainly caused because of fear of failure or getting dissatisfied and taking disruptive factors into consideration. So, the factors of the heart have to be detached from our controlling mechanism in case we detect any sign of stress. This keeps our system in stable position even with stress. The art of differentiation if applied properly can solve all these problems. It employs logical thinking and intuition to differentiate between various things like good and bad, right and wrong, our psychological status and so on.

4

Students' Strengths

Fortify the Powers

All power is within you; you can do anything and everything. Believe in that; do not believe that you are weak. Stand up and express the divinity within you.

— Swami Vivekananda

It is very important to discuss the strengths of the present day student. Knowing them in particular and in detail helps us in maintaining, strengthening them and using them. The strengths being discussed here are not individual strengths but the strengths in common to the students as a whole. Individual strengths are to be identified individually through self-analysis.

One of the most important qualities of a person is to identify ones strengths. Many times if asked of our strengths, we don't have an answer. That's where we start to lose. We can use a weapon only if we know that we have it and how to use it. Our weapons are there within us. There they are lying deep under the soil of time and innocence. Even Lord Hanuman was unaware of his powers for a long time. It is only when others told him that he remembered those supernatural powers. It is only then that he uses them in the right path and finds Goddess Sita and later to fight the evil and reuniting Ram and Sita.

Students' most important asset is their radiating energy. Just as Swami Vivekananda says, youth has a huge amount of energy bound in them. But the problem lies in identifying this power and using it.

One of the powers of the present youth is their hard work. The present day students are really hard working. But just as the huge amount of river water which goes into the sea leaving behind barren or flooded lands, most of their hard work is becoming waste. Most of the students just commit themselves to hard work without using their logical ability up to proper extent.

One should know the essence of hard work. It helps us a lot if used in a proper way. Understanding a particular concept can be done in some time by working on it. But going to the depths of it, understanding all the relative concepts, the way in which those are linked to the parent one, analysing its applications, limitations and advantages of the concept needs a lot of thinking and work to be done on it. This is called hard work.

To many of today's students, hard work means just spending hours before books and filling the memory with all the data and working for long time on the assignments. As the methodology of learning and the educational system act in the same way the students are not to blame. However, this material hard work is to be converted to a more quality one. Once it is converted to a more quality one, the student will be able to work better.

Imagination is another asset of our brain. Albert Einstein quoted 'imagination is more important than intelligence'. Imagination is really a great way to improve ourselves. We can use imaginative power in various techniques to improve concentration, relax the mind, improve thinking, and develop commitment, increase determination. And also imagination is a great asset in framing the theories and solving problems, especially in the technical aspects. The important principle on which these techniques are based is that, the world we live in is first made in mind and then is reflected onto reality.

I will explain how the concept of imagination helps us. It can be observed that the way we see each thing in our surroundings depends on the incidents we have had in the past and mostly, the recent past. Each person seeing the things in different ways is shows that the state of the mind or the past incidents affects the way of seeing the present incident. This means that the image a circumstance creates on one's mind changes from mind to mind or from person to person. If you observe this phenomenon carefully with a slightly a different orientation, it means that the images of the situations or the impressions of them are first created in our brain and then come into view when the situation is revealed. Here, I don't mean that images of each of the situation are created. I mean that a base is formed and the inclination of the mind to think in that particular way is formed. Most of these impressions are due to imagination and previous experiences. If you can control these impressions formed by the incidents, we can use them in various ways which are mentioned above. We can control the impressions by controlling the thoughts and imagining in a well-defined and positive pattern.

Faith is another important strength of us. More than strength, it is a need. A pure faith is the key to work efficiently. Absence of faith locks up our energies and disables us partially or completely. Faith is as sensitive as it is strong.

Faith is an ultra powerful element in us which forms a link between the heart and the brain. Faith is a resultant of the logic and reasoning of the brain and the feeling of the heart. However, in the case of faith, the brain plays less amount of the role than the heart. The role of the heart is the base and the role of brain is just to justify or validate it. Even here, the right balance between the heart and the brain is to be obtained as the faith gets unbalanced if either of them deviates from their proportions.

Faith is extraordinarily clear if it is pure and our view of it is clear. Faith being pure means the heart and the brain are maintained in the right proportions. The right proportions can be known through the greatest path of learning – intuition. I strongly believe we are more than we believe we are. We are stronger. We are more intelligent and we have more knowledge. But all of these are hidden deep in us waiting to be awakened. These hidden powers can be brought through the process of intuition. Many times, we tend to know things from inside. We feel that our inner mind is trying to tell us something. This is intuition. We have to listen to our inner brain. Here the heart and the brain get into optimal ratios. The thoughts in our consciousness which distort the heart-brain ratios don't affect this process as it happens completely in the sub-conscious mind. Learning through intuition is, listening to our inner mind or voice. This even helps us in understanding ourselves. Due to many external factors, we are suppressing our real self and are creating a virtual world in our brain. This is disabling our ability to listen to ourselves. It is becoming very difficult for us to listen to our inner voice and differentiate it from our regular thoughts. This voice is of utmost importance as it reveals us to us. It represents our real self.

From this, we can observe the importance of purity of faith. The source of faith is our inner self. And our view of faith means the way to accept, treat and apply faith. For this, the complete understanding of the concept of faith is a necessity. The complete understanding of faith can only be achieved through intuition.

Remember that faith is a highly powerful element. So, the faith shouldn't be blind. Blind faith may be destructive. Simply having faith in something or someone without proper logical line may mislead us. Even though faith is of the heart, we normally mistake blind faith to be pure faith. Logic is just to differentiate between the two, but it does not make faith. For example, consider the example of the faith in God.

God is everything and everywhere and is all powerful only if we have pure faith in Him, and, there is no God if we have no faith. It is not the God who helps us in need. It is in fact the faith in God that helps us in pulling us out of troubles. I would like to repeat the above sentence again for the sake of clarification. "It is in fact the faith in God that helps us in pulling us out of our troubles", but not, "It is in fact the faith in God that pulls us out of our troubles". Many people consider the second one. It is blind faith. The first sentence represents true faith. True faith is never alone. It is always accompanied with required work. But what does faith do when we work? Faith in ourselves, society and in the work we are doing gives us confidence, unleashes our inner energy and becomes one of the prime causes of doing the work. Many times we don't win a challenge or overcome a hurdle even though we put up sufficient work. This may be due to the lack of self-confidence, also known as faith in us.

Faith in Us

Having faith in us is a very important quality needed by us. Faith in us in the capability point of view is genorally known as self confidence. However, faith in us also consists of faith that we go in the right way, faith on our ability to differentiate and choose and so on. These can also be treated as a part of self confidencc in taking decisions. You can't even imagine of winning a struggle without faith. If you believe that your capability is less than needed, can you put as much as needed which in your point of view is more than your conceived capability? No! You don't believe that you are powerful to the required extent. You feel you are weak and that makes you really weak. And you lose faith further when you see the results obtained due to the partial effort. And cumulatively, it causes your fall.

Faith on the society means faith in our parents, friends, colleagues, teachers, and so on. Absence of any of these faiths has almost the same effect as in the previous case. We will be feeling lonely and will not be able to work with anyone if there is no faith. We will be under estimating them and this moves us away from working with them and listening to them.

Effect of Faith on Us

The effect of faith on us is highly above our point of perception. True faith with intuition helps us to unleash the inner energy required to do work. Similarly, faith in God helps us by remembering us that we are not alone in our fight and there is strong hand on our side. Working without faith is like working in the dark. Having bad faith means leaving ourselves to fate and not working to achieve our goal. It is dangerous. It should be very clearly understood that the role of faith is only to unleash our inner energy and not to do the work. Both faith and work in the required amounts together moves us towards the destination.

Scope

Which is more important – development or the scope for development? Development denotes the past or the present where as the scope for development denotes the future. Development is a limited thing where as its scope can be unlimited. Our rise or fall in the future in a particular field depends even on the scope we have in that particular field along with the work we put up for it. We can compare scope to potential and development to the result of that potential – analogous to current in electrical sciences, velocity in mechanics. Here the fundamental quantity is the potential. So, for setting our future course, we have to set the scope.

Many believe that the scope for development is determined solely by the external factors and development depends on our work (The external factors are the factors which are parameters of the society's effect on us). In fact, we are the prime determiners of the scope.

Ideally, scope is infinity. However, in many cases, we define things taking only the extent until which we can see them into consideration but not the extent they actually are.

Scope comes into the same category. The scope we consider to exist is just the amount of scope we realize but not the amount which actually exists. That means in the process of increasing our scope, we are not actually increasing the scope but are just increasing the scope existing in our view which can be called effective scope. However, in this book, I am referring even effective scope just as 'scope' to avoid the confusion.

But how can we realize scope? Realizing scope means redefining new limits and identifying new ways of development. We have to search for new possibilities. We have to create new paths. We have to search for new paths to realize our goals. We have to extend the virtual limits we have set for ourselves in a controlled manner. This can be done by taking the resources and other factors which affect in realizing our dreams. We have to work in the paths which in turn increase the scope we have in working in future. This aids our development in future.

5

Parents
The First Teachers

Too often we give our children answers to remember rather than problems to solve.

— Roger Lewin

It is well said that the parent is the first teacher. Most of the child's brain develops in his first days. During these days the child is not much influenced by external factors and the influence on the child is solely due to the parents. These days form the base of character and attitude on which the child builds his future. So parents contribute to a major part of the orientation of the brain of the child. The effect of the external factors and other relationships in turn depend on the relationships with their parents.

The importance of the role of parents arises due to the facts that they form the base of the entire child's framework of mind and that the children are sensitive to the environment. The duty of a parent is very tough. A child lives with his parents for most of the initial stages of life. But all the children are not very comfortable with their parents, even though they love their parents. Why is it so? The complications here arise because even though parents and child love each other and both work for the good of the child, their methods are different. There is always a lack of perfect synchronization between the two due to the dominative and traditional nature of the parent, modern and inexperienced nature of the child and generation gap. The challenge of a parent is to bring these two into synchronization.

This is a small encounter which I had encountered on my way to college. A friend of mine was saying to another "My parents said I had to work hard when I am in school so that I can score well in my exams. Then they asked me work hard to score well in board exams. After that they asked me to work hard in my intermediate as those marks may be important in getting a good engineering seat and in getting a job. Later they asked me to work hard so as to get a good rank in competitive exams as it governs the seat and college I get to pursue my engineering. And presently they are asking me to work hard so as to get a good job and keep up their expectations on me. And I am sure that it is going to continue." This is just one of the many similar incidents which happen frequently. This is another reason why the students just work hard and I don't think this is going to help the child in the least. What we can observe here is the way the student is vexed of studies and is pressurized by the parents. Why should it be so? And surprisingly it happens only in the case of education.

Most of the parents want to comfort their children and shield them from problems. But this is not a good practice. A child should be aware of the problems up ahead of him. Keeping him in comfort zones will deprive him of the qualities required to fight the problems. It is better to teach fish instead of giving a fish a day. Isn't it? For example, consider a family in which the father is very strict, may be due to the problems faced by him in the past or being faced by him in the present, and the mother is one who always tries to keep the child in the right path by scolding. What would happen to their child, let's say a boy? Due to the prevailing conditions at home, he may not be able to share his feelings. What then? At home he is strictly packed within some tightly bound limits. But outside, he has no limits applied by his parents. He will be his master. And he may become closer to his friends than the parents. Now consider the same situation with the boy having some siblings younger to him and was aware of the struggle of his parents to come to the present position. What happens then? He is aware of the struggle faced by his parents. So he may develop a special respect to them. He develops zeal to work hard and satisfy his parents and comfort them in future. So he has a reason to work hard which many miss. As he has some younger sibling/siblings, he understands that he should take care of them too. These help them in developing some positive qualities. A small difference of knowing the struggle of his parents is bringing about a huge difference.

Many children lose power to control themselves with time. Improvement is becoming declination. Those who at the age of 2 years were calm, listening to their parents, using their mind in positive way moved off the track and anger, started crying for everything, became more fearful, and started asking for things like chocolates increased at a rapid rate. (Understand the reason for this nature than just cutting it out as a normal childish behaviour). In most of the cases it is the small instances which are the governing elements. These small instances includes a child being less preferred by their siblings and playing with some others, a small fight between parents, parent warning the child of the dark and of a fictional element and fearing him to give to a stranger if he doesn't listen, and many more. These will sow the seeds of anger, frustration, inferiority or superiority complex, dominative nature, nature of taking advantage of a situation, and so on. A parent should know the fact that children are great observers and dissolves such things easily into sub-consciousness forever. Never doubt if a small incident does influence the brain. Any action of the brain is a cumulative result of all the incidents of the past. However, some actions may have more effect than others and the recent ones may have more effect than the older ones.

Another reason for the negative attitude of the child in some cases is the parent's tendency to scold the children, even if there isn't his fault or scolding illogically. Many children say that they get angry on elders only when they scold them even if he do no wrong or when they scold illogically. Scolding illogically means, scolding the child by linking unnecessary things and without proper logic.

There is a lot of effect of society on the parents and his/her way of dealing with the child. The effect of the society on a matured parent plays more prominent role in shaping of the child than its effect on a maturing child. Generally, most of the parents make their child follow the general trend of the society, compare with others, and put pressure on the child based on the society's factors and inputs. A child has to be isolated partially from the effect of the society by the parent. Parent has to filter the effect of the society and pass only those which are useful for him in the way he would want.

Parents many times feel the child is going in the wrong path just because it is not their way or is the way they are not aware of. A parent shouldn't have a doubt that the child is going in a wrong path. And if the parent is sure that the child is in the wrong path, the best time to set it all right is when he is at the start. The best way to bring the student into the right path is by making him realizing his mistake. Parents have to understand that the children may go in a different way which may be a good one. Parents have to understand the difference and analyse the child's way in that manner. Parents letting the child to be in his way solves half of the problems and the remaining half can easily be solved by the thus elevated relationship between them.

One of the prime factors to be considered while framing a good parent-child relationship is the child's attitude towards the parents. The child's attitude towards parents is delicately balanced between the parent's actions and the outside world. A child never dislikes his parents, but, most of them do get angry and frustrated towards his parents at times. There are many reasons for this. One of the reasons is, parents' general tendency to limit the child's actions and control him, of course with the thought of making them go in the right path. Most of the children feel it irritating and may rebound or take the suppression as granted and may go to depression with the aid of some other factors. I don't mean the parents have to let the child go completely in his own way. The parent instead of limiting the child has to channel the child's thought process and actions. Both of these are different. In limiting, the way which many parents follow, parents make the child do what the he feel is right not giving priority to the child's feelings. In case of channelising the child, the parents lets the child to go in his own path and just see that he will not go in the wrong path. Another important property of this method is the parent will just help, only if he is utter need, to bring the child out of problems but does not bring him out of his problems. The child will only be solving his own problems making him stronger and tougher for the future. In this method, the parent is a third person who monitors the child and helps him find his path.

One of the best ways parents can deal with a child is by reliving the childhood. They should place themselves in the child's position and have to think what he would do if he is in that position. For this the parent has to observe the child in the minutest way. Relive the past. Feel the way the child would feel in that situation. Think about the way the child wants the parent to be. Feel the joy you wanted to have when you were young. Think about the mistakes you have committed when you were young. Analyse them. Move with the world. Don't let the child go off his own grip. Make him learn the ways. Teach them the difference between the right and wrong. Find the cause of the child's trouble, if any. You don't force the child away from the problems neither solve them. Instead make him know the cause of the problem. Just monitor from the third person's position that your child don't get into deep trouble. Let him do mistakes. Make him realize the mistakes. Make him solve them. Remember that mistakes form the path to realization. It is the way that you have to teach but not the solution.

The parents have to maintain the right balance between the outer world and the environment at home. For example, if the teachers in school and the friends praise him of his good qualities and the parents doesn't bother about the positive qualities and continuously try to mend the negative ones or vice versa, the child may develop hatred, anger and may suppress himself to great extent. Similarly, the parents have to understand the struggle of the child in outer world through the day and the mental tensions he might possess. The parents shouldn't think neither should expect the child to be in the same mood everyday. The child is affected by the environment in the same degree as the elders are and may even be more as he is not much matured.

Parents have to keenly observe the child. They have to completely study, observe and analyse the effects of the external environment on the child. Unbiased analysis of the observation is a necessity. The parent should not approach with a biased attitude that the child will for sure be in the right path or with the doubt that the child is going into the wrong path. These conceptions bias the parents' judgment of the child. Wrong judgments impose emotional pressures on the child disturbing his stability. The parents should carry out the observations and analysis very systematically and should directly target the child's psychology. A parent should put himself in various shoes like a parent, the child's friend, a third person to analyse the child before coming to a conclusion. A parent has to observe the patterns and changes in the child's behaviour. A parent should observe if the child is trying to hide his usage of phone, if he prefers to stay alone, if he prefers to stay in the dark, if his interaction with the parents has reduced, if he is spending more time out of the house, if he is trying to hide something, and so on. Using phone more is not a problem but the child trying to hide is a problem. The child worrying about something is not much a problem, but it is to be given thought if it is so for long or is frequent. A child staying long outside is not a problem. But if he tries to escape from home, it is time for the parents to question themselves. Whenever the parent sense a problem with the child, the first thing to be done is seeing their role in creating the problem and then what the child can do to solve the problem and then the assistance the parent can give to the child.

My dear parents, I want to give you an advice. Never think to pull the child out of problems or to completely prevent them from problems. Instead train them to solve them on their own. Let them build their own steps to the future. I will tell you a small story which one of my teachers once told us. Once in a biology lab, the teacher was demonstrating the birth process of butterfly. The teacher then placed an egg on the table, asked the students to observe it for sometime and went out. Suddenly the egg started hatching and caterpillar started coming out off the shell. It is struggling a lot to come out of the shell. Seeing that, a child there pitied it and was hurt by the small insect's struggle. So, he decided to help it and slowly and carefully removed it out of the egg and placed it on the table. Just when the child started feeling pleased to have helped it, the insect struggled for some time and died! All were shocked of the incident. Just then the teacher came and explained the incident. The caterpillar has to struggle a lot to adjust to the surroundings of the outer world as it was accustomed to the conditions of the egg. So, it has to struggle and break the egg with its own strength and get accustomed to the comparatively harsher conditions of the outer world. As the student simply broke the egg and brought the caterpillar outside, he brought it out of the struggle for existence. Due to the sudden change of surroundings, the caterpillar was not fit enough to struggle. So the caterpillar which later develops into a beautiful butterfly, died instantly. Nature reveals such incidents abundantly. Tortoises lay few thousands of eggs in the sand of a sea shore. But barely a few reach the sea and survive there. Most of the eggs become preys and the tortoises becomes prey to the sea animals. The ones which struggle and win the battle of existence survive for as long as 120 to 140 years. Lord Jesus Christ was treated as a holy one because in spite of the great problems he faced, he stuck to his goal of spreading love and healing the mind of the people. This made him divine. Parents shouldn't protect the children instead they should encourage the child to solve them. Solving a problem in the present makes him capable of solving similar ones in the future. Developing on his own makes him fit to survive. Surely teaching fish is far better than giving fish, but teaching the way the fish and waters behaves in addition is the best.

A parent's role is completely satisfied only when the child can be his actual self both at his home and in the outside world. Previously children were closer to the family than to friends. But the time has changed the scenario. Children are not able to be their actual self with their parents which is the case with majority of the present children. The children have become closer to the friends than to the parents. The prime reason for this is the parent. It is the lack of their proper understanding of the child which is causing it. The society accepts as we are and it is we who sets the boundaries. But at home it is the parents who define the boundaries. Also, the changing external environment creates the scope for change which is not there at home. I don't mean the child should not be close to the friends. The parent has to move with time and act in synchronous with the external environment. Make the child believe you are there with them. Get the confidence in them. Dear parents, make the house a better home for the child. And my dear friends make the parents feel more secure.

6

Friends and Society

The Guides

"A friend is one that knows you as you are, understands where you have been, accepts what you have become, and still, gently allow you to grow."

— William Shakespeare

Friendship is one of the most important relationships. Friends are not just our companions in the outer world. They are our second teachers of life after parents and are as important as them. They are our guides in the world. The only difference between them is parents try to teach directly and the friends' teachings are embedded in their relationship. The parents play the role of forming the base and launching it upwards, friends help us to follow the intended trajectory. The greatness of society is they accept us as what we are. However, selecting and adjusting the limits between the friends is very important.

The effect of a friend may be positive, negative or both. Generally the effect of a friend is both positive and negative but frequently, negatives influence us more than the positives. A person affecting us in a negative way is not a person with all the negatives. It only means we are seeing the negative part of him. We have to deal the negatives of a friend separately and should not mix them with the positives. It helps us maintain the relationship. We have to carefully monitor ourselves and our friendship so as to prevent any possible negative effect on us.

The main role of friendship in building us is the maturity it develops in us. Friends teach and guide us through our life. They teach us what is right and what is wrong. They teach us how to behave with others and how to deal with situations. Friends are the best guides to maturity. Parents have experience but the conditions prevailing during their time and now are different. Friends know the prevailing situations. So we have to take inputs from both.

The effects of friends can be divided into six stages. The first stage includes the pre-school days. The role of friends in the childhood plays an important role in determining our approach to friends in the later part. It is the role of the parent to condition the relationship of a child with the friends in the childhood. Most of the children get attracted to the friends due to the similarities in the thinking, age, and moods. Due to this they get more oriented towards friendship and may tend to neglect other relationships. Some people are quite opposite to this. They develop some hatred or repulsion towards friendship. It may be due to harsh limitations imposed by parents, or due to quarrels with friends, or due to a sibling who do not give priority to him due to his attraction towards friends. Parents have to manage these. The children in this stage do not have the maturity to understand. So the parents have to create them. For example, if there is a small fight between two siblings, parents has to create the condition where they will like each other, or if the elder is matured, make him understand. And when they are together, amplify it. Just words don't do the job. It can even get the child into situation that 'mom says just like that all the time', when your word loses its value.

The second stage consists of the child joining of the school and the primary school days. Here the child may seriously start to deviate from his way. This is one of the turning points of the child. Here, the time the child spends with parents' decreases and the time spent with friends' increases abruptly. This is the time when the parent-child relationship plays an important role. It becomes one of the prime factors in determining the orientation of the child towards parents and other relationships. The parent has to monitor this transient period carefully and should cut the negatives in the starting itself.

The third stage is during the higher school education of the child. Here the bond with the friends becomes stronger. In some cases the disturbances at home may make that relationship weaker. Aiding to this, the monotonous nature of the school and education initiates the need of excitement in the children. All of these may act cumulatively resulting in deviation of the child. This can be avoided if the parent moulds the child initially or by making the child realize his mistakes.

The fourth stage is the senior secondary education or intermediate stage. This is the most volatile and uncontrollable state owing to the huge educational stress on the children in this state. The parent has to regulate the environment at home and see that the child doesn't deviate. But the influence of the parent on the child begins to weaken.

The fifth state is the graduation level. This is the final orienting level of children. This effect of this level may be negative or positive, both divided by a single line. We may go to the either side. Most of the students in this stage become highly matured. They undergo the transition from children to adults both socially and psychologically. They develop strength to face pressures and qualities to fight problems. This is the state where the relationship with the friends and parents attains more quality and strength. The main advantage with this state is that it is completely flexible and creates an environment in which one can change the way he wants. People learn lessons for life here which will be there with him through out his life. The friendship in this state is more pure and is the most effective. The role of friend attains clarity in this state. Here a friend shares everything from a small joy to great problem. The effect of a friend is also clearly visible here. People in this state try to mend others and grow into a better people. It is the mostly himself and his friends who influences the child. But if he doesn't properly monitor the affects, the negative results may be as much worse.

The sixth stage is the state after studies. There will not be much change from the fifth to sixth state in the friendship point of view. However, the maturity comes into play once more and moulds them.

Friendship is one of the most prominent relationships in our life. Initially, it is mainly dependent on other relationships. But slowly it becomes more independent from other factors and becomes self-dependent. Friendship affects our character, attitude, and other relationships greatly. The understanding nature of friends and similarities between friends adds strength to this relationship. We learn from friends, and they guide us. They are the ones who let us be whom we want to and keep our inner self alive. They are our source of inspiration. They are our companions for joy and our guides in problems.

7

Logical Thinking
The Essence

The mind is its own place, and in itself
can make a heaven of hell, a hell of heaven.

— John Milton (1608-1674), Paradise Lost

The brain is a monstrous, beautiful mess. Its billions of nerve cells-called neurons-lie in a tangled web that displays cognitive powers far exceeding any of the silicon machines we have built to mimic it.

— William F. Allman (from Apprentices of Wonder. Inside the Neural Network Revolution, 1989)

The very essence of education is to develop logic.

Logic is a tool to deduce things from available data through reasoning. The series of thoughts developed through reasoning can be called as logical maps. These are similar to the flow charts drawn by programmers. At each node (or thought), we take some fact or feeling or a reason as the controlling factor which decides the next thought through logic. The most amazing thing is the huge logical maps and the process is completed in a fraction of a second. We normally don't give any interest towards how our thoughts are being processed. That is the main reason why we fail to recognize whole of the map and are left with only the initial and the final thoughts.

The technique of retracing the thoughts proves this. If you observe any two thoughts just a few seconds apart when your brain is in an active mode or when you are thinking in a random way, they will, most probably, appear as if there is no link between them. Take two such thoughts which are apparently consecutive. Now, try to deduce each and every intermediate thought with the tools as reasoning, feeling and fact known. Go to the depths of each link and divide them to the minutest level. Satisfy yourselves completely by giving reason to every minute link. The most important rule of this exercise is, don't think of doing this exercise before selecting the thoughts. Just select the present thought and last thought which is well in your consciousness. While doing the exercise, observe the delicacy of reasoning and sensitive nature of thoughts. I am sure these will fill you with awe. This process will not only reveal the capability of your brain, but also help you in refining your process of building the logical maps. It will improve your intelligence, which, according to me, is the ability to develop logic maps.

But, how does education help in developing the ability in us to build logical maps? Education brings us into contact with various problems and their solutions. We will be able to work on a given data to get a solution. We learn to analyse things. The way we dealt with a situation in mathematics may be applicable in a completely different subject. Education gives us knowledge using which we solve a given problem. Far more importantly, we will learn how to deal with real life situations through education.

How to Develop Logical Thinking?

There are a few things in nature which have the special quality of increasing themselves on using. Knowledge, intelligence, character come into this category. Each time we apply logic, our ability to use it increases. The technique of retracing the thoughts is one of the techniques which serve multiple purposes. When you are practicing this technique you are decoding a logic map, beautifully framed between the initial and final thoughts. In this way, we are in turn using logic to reveal the delicate links. So, we are practicing logic. In this process of decoding, we will be again building more logic maps to find the link. So, we are slowly developing the ability to frame logic maps.

The above method develops the ability to develop logic maps from the inside. This method helps us to understand logic as we are actually going to the base of logic by developing the logical maps. There are some methods which develops just the ability to develop logic maps. By practicing these methods, we will develop the ability to develop logic maps, but we will not be able to understand logic. The advantage of these methods over the previous one is their easiness to practice. The previous ones are far deeper than they appear.

Some techniques of developing logic are just practicing logic by solving puzzles, playing, reading books, and so on. Also logic has to be learnt from mistakes we commit. Whenever you commit a mistake in your logic map, identify the mistake and correct it. Embrace mistakes as they are our best teachers.

Writing our analyses helps us a lot to think structurally. While writing we think in a more orderly fashion and we get a chance to monitor ourselves. When you want to analyse yourself, sit alone and write your thoughts. You needn't show it to anyone. After completion, just close the paper. Repeat the same the next day and compare the two thought processes. You will understand the way you think and also the faults in your thought process. If you apply the same by writing your positives and negatives, it helps in self-analysis.

For application of logic in a proper manner, we have to build up a very strong thought process. Our thought process should be very strong, structural, flexible and efficient. A thought process is our generalized way of approaching a problem. Most of the people don't build their thought process consciously. In such cases, the thought process builds itself depending on various factors. This may cause lack of control of the thought process. Building our thought process consciously makes us better.

Developing the thought process consciously from the starting is a very tough process. The better and more practical method is identifying our mistakes in applying logic and identifying the possible logic paths we are missing and correcting our mistakes. By correcting our approach, we are building a better thought process in a better way. It is regenerative in nature. Analyse your thought process through the retracing the thoughts method and analyse your actions, identify your mistakes, correct the thought process, recheck it. That's the process, simple and straight forward.

Our thought process has to be well structured. But what is meant by a structural way of thinking? A level by level hierarchical way without missing any links is called structural thinking. Most of the people follow what I call as off-the-base thinking. In this mode, the thinking is not level by level and there will be no perfect links between the initial and the final points. In the case of solving a problem, the off-the-base thinkers just see the initial and final points, i.e. the outline of the problem and the possible result after solving the problem, but do not see the intermediate links, the solution of the problem. A good thinker does not miss any node and form perfect links between them using logic. The problem with off-the-base thinking is we tend to deviate from logic path.

Understand logic, apply logic and improve logic. That's the rule!

8

Controlling the Mind Energy

Tame the Shire

Cultivation of mind should be the ultimate aim of human existence.

— Dr. B. R. Ambedkar

The perfect establishment of control of mind energy is essential to prevent any deviations (leakages) and to use the brain effectively. Before coming to control of our mind energy, we have to first know about the mind energy. The heart and the brain are the two entities of us. While heart feels, mind works on logic. Neglecting heart and giving more priority to mind will make us miss the key factor – happiness and relations. This in turn affects our working efficiency. Giving more priority to heart will sway us away from logic path. Balancing these both is important. At the same time we need to tune both of them to satisfy our need. This is controlling the mind. Heart is uncontrollable but the effect of heart can be controlled by the mind.

We, the youth, has tremendous amount of energy bound in us. As there is such a great amount of energy, the control over the energy should be as much powerful. This is what most of the youth lack. First of all they don't believe that they possess such energy. Even if they believe, most of them don't identify it. Even if they identify it, they don't see the path of using it. But what is this energy. Energy here doesn't mean just physical energy to do physical work. It is the mental energy.

It is not an easy task to identify this energy. It is said that no tiger is a man-eater by birth. It is only when it tastes the human blood that it becomes mad and it starts hunting people for feasting on their flesh. Similarly, no human tastes this energy nor identifies it initially. But once he tastes that energy, he will be in continuous pursuit of this energy. Believe in this, once you identify the bounded energy in you, you will be filled with awe, an ultimate awe of realization and satisfaction. Once you think of that energy, you will be filled with an unknown combination of emotions filled with happiness, awe, satisfaction and a tremendous confidence. Ah! One has to identify it at least once. What a great feeling it is! It takes you off this world. You can practically feel some energy in your body. Your body will be radiating with energy.

Somo explain this as the cosmic energy or as god's energy. We can't say a particular explanation to be right and others are wrong. According to me, the concept of religion and the modern science are two different explanations given to the working of the nature. Both of these conceptual schemes have their own pattern of thought and both of them have formed their own bases. In the concept of religion, an external, ultra-powerful source of energy and controller – god – is considered as the base. In modern science, few theories like the conservation of energy, structure of atom, theory of gravitation, and so on form the base. Religion uses faith as tool more than logic and contrary to this, modern science uses logic more than hypothesis. The validity of one of them does not invalidate the other conceptual scheme. Both of these belong to two different dimensions and hence we can't say a particular version is right. We can believe in one or both of them. We can clear the confusion by treating both of them as two different things unlike the normal perception that both of them are complementary and rivalries.

The only way to use this energy is by identifying it. The more you feel it, the more you will be in touch with it. Did you ever identify it? Did you ever feel that you are radiating with energy when you are seriously working on some problem? Did you ever feel the presence of some unknown energy in you when you discuss some topic which is of great interest to you in a very lively way? Did you ever find some energy passing through your nerves when you meditate in solace? Did you ever feel the inner happiness when you achieve something on which you worked hard? This is the energy. It is hidden in us waiting for it to be used.

Even science is proving that the capacity of our brain is more than we actually thought. Previously, it is believed that the capacity of our brain is of the order of about 3 gigabytes. Later, it is estimated the brain's memory storage capacity to something closer to a 100 gigabytes. But now some of the researches show that it is close to 2.5 petabytes (or a million gigabytes). Why is it that the people didn't expect it before? Why the capacity of the brain is estimated less before? Is the capacity of the brain increasing by time? Are the brains of the present generation more powerful?

Previously it was believed that the sky is a concentric sphere at a finite distance from the earth. Later it was identified that it is not so and they thought that the whole of the space is what all we see. But it was later discovered that it is not so. The space is vast. The universe is vast. It is ever expanding. Does this mean that the universe was like the way our early ancestors thought sometime ago and it later changes? No! The universe is like that all the time. What had changed is the way we look at it. In the same way, our brain is always vast. What had changed is the way we see it. The way we see had changed because we started to use the brain more. We developed more ways of using our brain. We developed a huge number of subjects on which we can work on. This developed the capacity, rather the amount of the capacity of our brain we use or realize.

But what are we to do to use it? The first and foremost pre-requisite of using this bounded energy is to believe that there is such an unidentified energy in you. The story on Lord Hanuman applies even here. Take this fact to the heart. Always find ways in which this faith increases. Remember that it is the faith that can win all the energies. The next step is to develop the faith in ourselves. It is important to have faith in yourselves that you can release the energy from the deepest blocks of your brain. It is important that you proceed to next steps only if you are strong in the pre-requisites. It is only when the base of a building is strong that the building is strong. Even a small doubt in the presence of energy or your ability to unleash acts as a blockade and will resist you from releasing that energy.

Remember the symptoms which I mentioned where we will feel the energy. Do you find any common in those situations? In these situations you are focusing on a particular task without letting any other unrelated factors affect you. Neither is you thinking what you should do after that particular task. Neither is you thinking what others are feeling about you. You are solely concentrating on the present. This is what is actually releasing the energy. Focus and work on a task with concentration.

Another good way to bring the energy to the surface is by feeling its presence. Feel the presence and the flow of the energy in each of your veins. Feel the energy in the muscles. Lie down peacefully. Concentrate on each of your muscles and try to release the tightened ones. Make them relax. Start from the toe and feel each part. Relax the toes, legs, fingers, arms, hands, neck, eyes and so on. And at last come to the brain. Work on it at peace. Don't worry about the time. Slowly you will start feeling the presence of the energy. This method has an additional advantage. Your body will be getting some pure relaxation. Each or at least most of the muscles relax. At the end you will find yourself full with energy. Never satisfy with what you achieve this time. Realize that each time you do this exercise, relaxation obtained increases. Realize that each time you do this; you relax your muscles much better than the previous time. Each time you will find that the energy you are observing is more than the previous time. This means that you are releasing the energy. Do this exercise with utmost concentration and don't let any external stray thoughts effect you.

The process until now is releasing the hidden energy. All this energy becomes useless if we don't know how to use it. The way we use the energy and the extent we can use it depends on how we frame our thoughts and how we control the energy. We have to frame a way to use this energy. Once started doing the exercise of releasing this energy, we have to continue it. Any gap in doing the exercise would bring our state back to the start. When we just fall a little, other pressures of the society will make us fall more. So, once started, we have to take it to the end. Even if we unknowingly or knowingly had to break the chain, we have to realize our fault and start again. Another important rule is that we have to use all or at least most of the energy. As we know that energy can't be stored but just can be converted from one form to another. If we have caused some small gap in the process, it may result in a huge damage. After reaching some particular stage, having no control over the released energy may cause a great damage to our mental stability. This is because, when the energy is generated – or rather released – it should be used. So, a perfect control has to be setup during the course of our up-gradation. A steady growth has to be aimed against a sudden growth.

Our brain is simply worth many super computers. We have such an energetic brain. And we are not using it. I want to stress one thing here. 'We are not using it' but it is not that 'we are not able to use it'. What only if we can completely control the thoughts? Isn't it great? This is a part of controlling mind energy.

Concentrating is one major part of controlling the brain.

When Swami Vivekananda, was living in Chicago, USA, he used to go to the library, borrow large volumes of books, take them home and return them the next day. After some time the librarian became curious and asked him, "Why do you take out so many books when you can't possibly read them all in one day?" Swami Vivekananda replied that he read each and every page of every book. The librarian could not believe it, and so Swami Vivekananda asked her to test him. She opened a book, selected a page and paragraph, and asked him to tell her what was written there. Swami Vivekananda repeated the sentence exactly as it was written in the book, without looking at it. The librarian was astounded and did more tests. Each time Swami Vivekananda repeated the exact words written in the book. (Source: Enhancing the Ability to Study, Swami Niranjanananda Saraswati, Talk to school students aged 14-17 years in Kolkata, September 2004). Then Swami Vivekananda explained that it is by concentration and practice that he is able to do that. He explained that as a child, we first read letter by letter and after some time, we will be able to read a word at a time. But with much practice and concentration one can read a whole sentence and even a whole page at a single glance. He is a perfect example of what a person, especially the youth, can do with the power of concentration.

What else does controlling the mind constitute of other than concentration? Concentration means paying attention onto a particular thing. But controlling the brain also constitutes, keeping the brain in proper position even when we are not doing any work and also making up our brain to do some work.

But how should we develop this control over our mind? Here, I discuss some very effective techniques, but, the best method is, we have to create our own ways to use this mind energy.

One tool is Music. Listen to music and follow the pitch and oscillate with it. This not only improves our concentration power, but also helps us check our status. Meditation is not just sitting in a quiet place and concentrating on our breath. This type of meditation is a highly efficient one. But we can use similar techniques to create a similar impact on us. When our aim is to improve concentration, why can't we do it in some other way which even though is far less efficient, is more reliable and easily accessible. When we train our brain to concentrate on some particular thing, it becomes a habit. We can develop many other techniques to develop our control. We have to continuously monitor ourselves and identify where we are lacking control over our mind. For example, sometimes we slip and our actions go beyond the limits we have imposed on ourselves. We have to identify such situations and have to tighten the limits and be stronger onto self to prevent deviation.

Breathing technique is another wonderful technique. By controlling our breath in different ways, we can control different states of our brain ranging from attaining concentration and settling our mind, to suppress, divert anger, and to bring us out of depression. Regulating breath means regulating inhaling and exhaling. These can be easily obtained by practice and through trail and error method.

Minimizing Deviation

Minimizing deviations is an important part to keep our mind in control. To minimize the deviations, we have to first understand ourselves and then about the factors which affect us.

These factors which affect us can be classified into two types – internal factors and external factors. Internal factors are the factors which are the characteristics of us like our feelings, attitude, and so on. The external factors are factors affecting us from the environment which influence through various means like the society, educational system, and so on. The external factors cannot be controlled, but the effect caused by them on us can be controlled. The internal factors, however, will be in turn affected by the external factors. It is very important to control the internal factors which are essential for controlling the affect caused by the external factors.

The external factors keep changing continuously due to the change of relative environment. Due to this, the effect caused by them is also changing, even though the type of effect may be same. To deduce the type of the effect and the effect an external factor on us, we have to identify and analyse it. The external factors are detectable. A detected external factor is a very effective link to find the effect caused by it.

To detect the external factors and analyse them, we have to first understand ourselves completely. To start this step, we have to first remove the false impression that we understand ourselves completely, even if you think the impression is not false. This creates the required void in us which is an essential factor. The presence of such a void in our brain creates necessity to understand ourselves.

The external factors play their role in shaping us. These factors are similar to friction. Friction opposes the motion but more importantly is the cause of it. For example, we would not be able to walk if there is no friction. If you doubt it, try walking on a surface with less friction like an oily surface. Vehicles cannot stop when brakes are applied without friction. But is friction always useful? It is due to friction that huge amount of energy is being wasted. The friction being an advantage or a disadvantage depends on the application and intensity of friction. External factor aiding or hindering us depends on the factor, our attitude of taking it in and our state of mind.

An external factor may be useful or may oppose us. The effect of an external factor can be controlled by modulating it with reasoning and reacting in a proper manner. By this, we will be setting the friction needed by us in a particular situation. This filters the negative effects of the external factors. Generally, we get a lot influenced by the external factors. Whatever may be the circumstances we should work in our own way, rectifying it wherever needed, while balancing the environment and changes in it. The effects of these external factors have to be filtered and some of them are to be nullified to keep our system stable. Some people get highly influenced by one or two persons. Getting over influenced may also pass their negative qualities to us. The better and controlled way to get influenced is by filtering and taking all the good qualities which are suitable to us from every person.

The main problem faced by a person while minimizing the deviations is identifying that he is deviating. Most of the people fail to sense the deviation. The fundamental reason for this is we are accustomed to compromise ourselves! We say we are in the right path doing the right thing, but, we don't question ourselves if we are so. We are blindly going without checking ourselves. The only solution to this is confession. We have to confess about ourselves to ourselves. We brought us to that state and now, we have to correct ourselves.

Another important way to control the mind is by slowing it down. Due to the speed of the modern world and lack of proper control system, our thought process is too fast to keep our brain stable. We have to slow it down at least sometimes to bring it towards stability. Meditation is one way to do it. Slowing down doesn't mean to do the things in a slow manner. We have to slow down our pace of thinking at times and can get back at a steady rate after sometime. It gives us the scope to control even when we are back at full pace.

We will be under our better control only when we are on a rough plane. When we are on a smooth plane, we may lose our control and slip. We can use this to create a similar impact on our lives. We have to learn control in our hard times.

9

Converting Negatives into Positives
The Change

> Only one who devotes himself to a cause with his whole strength and soul can be a true master. For this reason mastery demands all of a person.
>
> **— Albert Einstein**

To improve ourselves, we have to reduce our negative qualities and improve our positives. For this, we have to convert our positives into negatives. Converting negatives into positives is really a great technique to improve our character and mental status. I simply enjoy doing this and take it as a game. For this we have to know first ourselves completely. We have to know our strengths, weakness and the way we are presently capable of handling the situations.

Converting negatives into positives can be done in two ways. In the first way, we should use the negative qualities we possess to produce a positive effect. The product of two numbers will be positive not only when, both are positive but also when both are negative. We are going to employ this here. Confused? For example, sometimes we get the right answer of a problem but still we find that we did some mistake in some step of the problem. That is because the effect of this mistake is compensated with some other mistake in some other step which together brings us the right result. This is the most basic principle of this method. We have to learn and develop techniques which use our negative points to get a positive result.

The second method of converting positives to negatives is by first completely removing the negatives and then making them positive. This method is like removing the weeds from the farm and replacing them with some useful plants. The previous method is like placing these plants in such a way that they will protect the good plants and use them to feed the cattle. The critical part of the first method lies in selecting the weeds to be removed and those to be placed to protect the main ones and selecting the place to plant them and way to use them. The critical part of the second one lies in carefully removing the weeds without leaving their traces and placing the good ones and taking the care of them. The previous one may not hold for all the cases but the second one holds good for all the cases. But the first will have some supplementary advantages. The previous one demands tactics and careful dealing, this one demands strong determination and harsh fight even against the heart.

Looking both the faces of the coin is important. Seeing both the positives and negatives of a problem or work at your hand is very important. The positives show us what we can achieve by doing the work and negatives show what not to do. Simply they together are needed to form a strategy of work. Similarly we should look anything in both positive and negative way. By looking in the positive way, we will develop hope and faith and by looking in the negative way, we will be able to expect the possible consequences and obstacles and will be able to prevent them. And if they are inevitable, we can make ourselves ready to face them.

Once, just before exams, my friend commented that he wanted to score 80 per cent. But he said he is not confident of scoring it and would score far less than this. This is what I told him. "Now you are going to enter a fight. This is a war between your capability which is far above your expectation and your lack of confidence. It is a war between the lack of confidence in your heart and capability of your mind. The target and zeal to score 80 are your arms. Now it's your turn to fight the war and my turn to see what is actually going to win, your heart or your mind". He replied, "even if I reach my target or not, one part of me is winning and the other is loosing so, I needn't worry about the result". I said, "Exactly. One is going to win and the other is going to lose. But which is going to win is the thing which matters. If you let the heart win, you are encouraging the negative quality, lack of confidence. And if you let the mind win, you are encouraging your positive quality of thinking and capability. It is up to you to decide if to encourage the positive quality or the negative quality. It is up to you how you accept the negatives in you." We dealing with positive or a negative quality depend on our attitude.

10

Self-analysis
Reveal the Secrets

The heart holds answers the brain refuses to see.

— Kall

Your work is to discover your world and then with all your heart give yourself to it.

— Buddha

No man was ever so much deceived by another as by himself.

— Fulke Greville

The.most important part of building a better us is monitoring ourselves. A closed loop control system is more accurate than an open loop control system. This is the property which shows the importance of self-analysis. To keep ourselves and our brain in control, we have to continuously take feedback, process it and rectify the errors. This process of taking feedback, processing it and analysing the various related factors is called self-analysis.

But, why do we need a concept called 'self-analyses'. Don't we know ourselves? Just for a change, let's ask ourselves these questions:

Do we know us really well or are we just cheating ourselves? If we really do, why do we feel something is pulling us back when we think so? What are we interested in? Are we satisfying our interests? Do we know our strengths and weaknesses? Then why are we not able cross many hurdles by properly using them? Do we really like the work we do? Then why do we get frequently bored or frustrated of it?

To understand 'Self-analysis' we have to understand what affects our character and our actions. As differentiated before, there are two types of factors which affect us – the internal and the external factors. The external factors cannot influence us directly but they need a channel to exercise control over us. Lapses in our mental system provide this channel. Without the faults in our system, the external factors cannot affect us. For example, the British could not take over India without the support of Indians, most of these who betrayed their own rulers. Similarly, an effect of an external factor over us denote that there is an internal factor supporting it, be it be a positive or negative effect. The positive effect is encouraged by a positive internal factor and a negative effect is caused by some negative in us. So, it is very important to control the internal factors for controlling the effect caused by external factors.

The external factors change continuously with time due to the change of relative environment. Due to this, the effect caused by this is also changing even though the type of effect is generally same. So, to deduce the type of effect and the effect caused by an external factor, we have to identify and analyse it. The external factors are uncontrollable. But, they are detectable and their effect on us is completely controllable. The detecting of an external factor is very important to keep our brain in control.

There are three ways to do self-analysis. In the first way, we are to ask ourselves, our inner self, about the way we are going. We have to check ourselves frequently. This is a direct process. We analyse ourselves from inside and correct ourselves. Even though this is a very effective technique as it changes us from inside, it is difficult to implement it effectively. The problem with this method is reaching our inner self is difficult and sometimes, we may let the heart interfere thereby biasing our process.

The second method is analysing us through our actions. This is easier and more practical because we analyse through our actions and needn't go to our inner self. The main difficulty in the previous is thereby not present here. This helps us to heal from the external part to the inner part. Our actions denote what we are inside. Our feedback here is our actions. We have to continuously check if what we are doing is right or wrong and correct our mistakes. This method requires continuous effort. In the previous method, we are tending to change from inside. That means we generally tend to do things correctly. In this method, initially, we may not think about the things correctly, but, we correct them before implementing it. The previous method is better but with continuous effort, both can heal us in the same manner.

The third method is treating yourself as a third person and talking with yourself. This method is similar to the first except that, 'what are my mistakes' becomes 'what are your mistakes. Respond to yourself. It needn't be directly talking to yourself. Write a letter to you or record what you want to tell to you and listen to it or text and chat with you. Question yourself, shout at yourself, cool yourself and answer yourself. This is a very effective technique.

I recollect my Telugu teacher say that there is no need for the old great sages to check the grammar when they write huge epics. Once they start writing, the meaning starts making its own way. The same happens even in our case. For example, when we were small we have to check our words so as to speak correctly. But as we grow up, we develop a skill of speaking without the need of continuous checking. This comes through continuous and non-retreating efforts we put forth to learn how to speak. Similarly, we needn't continuously check on ourselves once we train our mind to be in that way innately. Then, self-analysis becomes a part of our sub-conscious mind and a part of us.

11

Ideal Student

The Vision

> Let us think of education as the means of developing our greatest abilities, because in each of us there is a private hope and dream which, fulfilled, can be translated into benefit for everyone and greater strength for our nation.
>
> **— John F. Kennedy**

Ideal. What does it mean? Does it refer to the best? Does it refer to the point beyond which there can be no more improvement? Or is it the ultimate thing which anyone can achieve? Or does it refer to something existing only as a mental image or imagination? In my view, ideality shows the path. An ideal person, an ideal machine, an ideal state – all of these shows the paths which produce the best or the most accurate results with full efficiency. An ideal machine is that which has no losses and gives complete accurate results with no errors. But what is it in case of people? Ideality is relative. For example, we can say an ideal person is one with all of the good qualities and no bad qualities. But, what are good and what are bad qualities? What may be good for me may be bad for you. Good, bad, correct, wrong, ideal, non-ideal, are relative. They may vary from one to other.

Who is an ideal student? Is he the one who scores full marks in all the exams and can answer any question? An ideal student should have all the qualities of an ideal person along with a few other qualities. Here, I put forward only those additional qualities and a few of an ideal person.

The most important quality is maintaining a proper heart-brain relationship. This is a common property of an ideal student and an ideal person. This property is the most important one as it is the prime determiner of other critical factors like attitude, thought process, and character. This is also the most critical part due to the highly vulnerable and delicate natures of the heart, brain and the relationship between them. Attaining a proper and optimal heart-brain relationship can partially be done using the previously mentioned techniques. These will not set the relation in the right proportions, but helps us in controlling it and the related entities and parameters. The process of setting up proper heart-brain relationship can't be expressed in words. This process is a self learned one. A common approach for all the people will be invalid. Each person has different levels of sensitivity and magnitude of heart and the brain. This is due to the different surroundings they live in, situations they encounter, and a few other factors. Another important point to be noted is the optimal proportions of heart and brain vary with situations. In some cases, the heart is to be given importance and the brain in some other. The proper setting of the relationship helps us in taking proper decisions and in tackling the situations in a proper way.

Attitude is the next important factor. It is the way of how a person views a situation and people. Attitude setting is thus a necessity for a person. Setting the heart-brain relationship in a proper way and developing a proper thought process play an important part in setting our attitude. Ideally, our attitude on any thing before analysing it should be neutral. This prevents the biasing of our thought process.

The most important feature of an ideal student is his unlimited zeal to learn things through interest just for the sake of the attaining knowledge while simultaneously satisfying the material needs. A student should read for the sake of knowledge in the 'art for art's sake way'. He should work with zeal and passion for knowledge. In other words, his aim should be to satisfy his desire and to quench his thirst of heart to learn things. This sends him in pursuit of knowledge. However, this is not sufficient for the society as it looks up for material things like marks, percentage, ranks and jobs. An ideal student should be satisfying his personal interests and the society's measuring parameters in parallel. So, he should even work for marks. Most of the students fail here and give more priority to marks due to external pressures. But, they fail to recognize that by doing so, they are loosing the role of heart thereby becoming emotionally weak internally. Balancing both the ways is to be continuously monitored. Each of them should be given priority at different times in different situations.

Whatever may be the circumstances, a person should work in his own way while balancing, but not opposing, the environment and the changes in the relative environment by making some changes in his way wherever needed. Here, environment is our relationship with the family and society. Generally, the influence of the external factors on a person is very high. The effects of the external factors are to be filtered and nullified to keep our system stable.

We having our target or future vision and the ideal person we want to be in our mind shows us the way we have to mould ourselves. Without it, we will be a person roaming in the desert having no idea about his location. Having the ideality in our mind is thus a must. Along with this, we should also be continuously checking, correcting, reforming and upgrading it to make it more suitable to us. Also, we should not limit ourselves to the level which we think is the ultimate or the most practical thing. We should always aim for a level just an inch about the level we fixed as the ultimate one. It keeps us moving.

12

Ideal Education System

Unattainable?

Don't teach the students but create the environment in which they learn.

— Albert Einstein

The function of education is to teach one to think intensively and to think critically. Intelligence plus character - that is the goal of true education.

— Martin Luther King, Jr.

If you tell people where to go, but not how to get there, you'll be amazed at the results.

— Gen. George Patton

While an ideal student is one who will be able to work in any system, an ideal education system should be able to satisfy all the students in any situation. The present system has evolved over a few thousands of years and is a deeply rooted one. Just like any other system, it has both advantages and disadvantages. These are to be first analysed to build a better system. The advantages are to be maintained and improved while the disadvantages and problems are to be rectified. Additional things are to be added wherever needed. This is what makes a better system. The present system is too deep rooted to make such changes instantaneously. Another problem is that the society is not willing to change the system even if they are fully aware of the problems with the present system. Even if some people are willing to, they are not consistent. Here, I am trying to put forward the characteristics of a better system.

The main advantage of the present system is the scope it has created. The resources present in the modern world like the internet, huge number of books, access to highly experienced faculty, and so on. More than these, the developments in the existing streams and the development of many more streams are raising the standards of the education. We now have more paths to develop than at any time in the past. Along with the scope in the streams of study, the present system also has more scope in the way of study and is also able to expose the students to the outer world.

The most troubling factors of the present system are the stress it has created and the mode of evaluation of a student. The effect of the stress on the brain and the character of the student are already discussed before. However, it is to be observed that the stress is different from strain. Stress is the resultant of many external factors whereas strain is our response to stress. The student can minimize the strain of his brain and heart. However, the educational system has its part to play in minimizing the stress on the student it has created through the way of evaluation and the way of teaching the student.

The new system has to provide time for the students for themselves. The free time students get in college play a very important role. It brings down the level of stress and increases the interest of the students over education. Without this free time, the students' brains get strained under the heavy stress. Also, it doesn't get sufficient relaxation and hence cannot work with high efficiency and concentration. Providing free time not just relaxes the students' brains but also improve their efficiency and concentration. It would be better to teach for 7 hours and give one hour break than to teach for 9 hours. Most people think that by doing so, the students will just waste time. But the truth is the students try to escape from the system only because of the lack of free time. Give them one hour a day completely for themselves and they will surely reorganize them and divide time optimally between enjoyment and study.

In some cases, the present system is continuously fluctuating. For example, the stress on the students is very high just before the exams and is quite low in the normal days. Proper methodology is to be designed to reduce these fluctuations. This continuously fluctuating system is to be changed into a constantly increasing one. A constant increase in the stress develops the ability in the students in handling the stress, which in the previous case is a little low.

The students should also be made aware of the objectives of the syllabus and the system. This makes them learn better. As a simple example, learning a mechanical subject may seem ridiculous for an electrical student. But the students have to be made aware about the practical significance of the subject. Similarly some believe the wastage of learning social at school level when they are willing to become an engineer or a doctor. The reason for learning all of these has a lot of psychological and social importance along with the academic importance. Learning these subjects develop social maturity in us and without these it is difficult to live in the society. In the psychological point of view, these contribute a lot to the development of the attitude and thinking of the student. Similarly the method of teaching should also be changed as discussed in the second chapter.

There should also be psychiatrist available for analysing and helping the students and teachers. Teachers should also be given proper training to be able to observe the children.

The new educational system should be a path for the students to learn. The present system is more concentrating on filling the student's brain with all the stuff. This is making the students less capable in future. The system should teach the students to learn, as Albert Einstein once said, 'Don't teach the students. Just create the environment in which they can learn'. It is to some extent similar to the famous saying, 'teach fish but don't give fish'. But to be more accurate, it is 'Teach the way to learn fishing. It makes them learn anything'.

13

The Framework of Mind

The Inner Us

"Every problem is a gift - without problems we would not grow."

— Anthony Robbins

Sometimes the situation is only a problem because it is looked at in a certain way. Looked at in another way, the right course of action may be so obvious that the problem no longer exists.

— Edward de Bono

The Framework of Mind is an integrated system of the heart, the brain, their relationship, principles, ethics, and so on. Simply, it is the complete structure of our inner self. You can think it as our soul. Until now, we considered heart, brain, their relationship and thought process as distinctive elements. But in reality, them are a part our integrated system. We have to regulate all of them and create a proper link between each of them. We have to maintain proper balance between each of these for better overall performance.

The things discussed until now are a part of a larger integrated system – The Framework. Every action of us and every change in us affects every part of the system and more importantly the whole of the system. So, we should not try to change one part of it without analysing its effect on the whole system. In fact, we should stop talking about elements individually when we are dealing with whole of the system.

What we need to have is a strong, well-structured, unbiased, systematic and stable Framework of Mind. If we don't have it, we need to build it.

We need a set of rules and limits to govern our system. They are the principles and ethics we frame. They define our boundaries. The set of principles is our preamble. We can call our system to be strong only if we have strong principles and ethics and we stick to them. We have to implement and control the framework to satisfy our principles. These include our faith in various things, the limits we had set for ourselves, our definitions of good and bad. Frame some strong principles like 'Never let down myself', 'Identify the interests of the heart and work for them', 'never leave my interests', 'I have to work for the sake of myself and for the sake of society', 'Whatever may be the external forces, don't lose my principles', 'be hard to change thyself if I ever do any mistake', 'Never hate or think bad about something'.

Well-structured means following an order. Even though we use different logic in different situations, we follow a particular method of approaching a problem. Our basic format of approaching a problem is called our structure of thinking. Even if we feel we think in a random manner, we innately do have a structure of thinking or pattern of thinking. To build a better structure we have to rectify the faults in our structure. We have to identify where we are going wrong and follow proper mechanisms to correct them. We have to identify where we go wrong each time we do some mistake and correct it. We have to follow a step by step approach to a problem. It is opposite to the off-the-base thinking discussed previously. A step by step approach means going node after node through proper reasoning. This helps us in going in the right path as it makes us to thoroughly follow logic. We should miss no node or link. At each node, we have to search for all the possibilities and weigh them against each other and choose those which are most probable according the situation. Sometimes we have to follow more than one possibility, especially in the cases where we don't know what the result is likely to be, like when we are searching for a solution of a problem. Then all the possibilities are to be considered along with their probabilities. But when we have the idea of the destination we have to reach like in case of analysing a particular thing, we needn't consider all the possibilities. We have to check the possibilities and probabilities and weigh them against the situation and select the most possible ones. Sometimes, we tend to neglect those possibilities which we feel are very less probable. If we are in lack of all the data needed, they are to be considered we are sure until there is no probability, because they may have much more probability than we perceive in the starting.

For our thinking to be in the right path, we have to be completely unbiased. We have to be perfectly neutral. Doing so helps us in taking wise decisions. It helps us to see the problem exactly as it is without any amplification of the negative factors and the attenuation of the positive ones or vice versa. For example, let us say there is a big, complex problem in front of you. Improper heart-brain relationship builds fear, anxiety and tension in you where as a proper heart-brain relationship helps us in approaching the problem in a right way. This prevents unnecessary stress. This helps us make an optimal use of our tools and resources. Most of us fail here. Generally, heart dominates and causes the fear of the problem, stress, and causes instability. This partially paralyses our brain hindering it from working properly. Thus our brain doesn't work exactly in time of need. Inaccurate analysis is another problem we face during decisions. If we approach a problem biased with a possible solution in mind, we assume that our assumption is right and work only in that way. This blinds us of the other possible paths.

Our framework should be systematic. As the name suggests, we should deal with situations methodically. We have to deal with the different elements of the framework and the changes in them using a protocol which ensures accuracy. When we have a situation to deal with, we have to first check the principles and ethics to analyse it and set the heart-brain relationship accordingly. This ensures that we go in a proper path without deviation. Then we have to analyse the problem in an unbiased way in various perspectives and form all the possible causes and future consequences of the situation. We have to prioritize what we have to deal with first. Then we have to frame strategies to deal with them. The next step is to validate the strategies and select the best and checking the principles in parallel. Then implement it and review the results.

We have to employ various tools and techniques which help us in doing complex things in an easier manner. For example, 'The art of differentiation' is a tool with which we can differentiate between various things like right and wrong, good and bad, the various paths we possess. Using this art we can redefine many critical things. Using this tool we can differentiate between various things ranging from the common case to differentiate between correct and wrong and differentiating between good and bad, to the delicate cases where we have to select a link at a node (thought) among various others in a logic map where choosing a different link would produce completely different results and to solve some critical problems.

One application of the art of differentiation is related to goals. Most of us have goals. But do we have a good goal set by considering all the practical factors? We often fail to differentiate between goals and derived goals. Goals are what we want to be whereas; derived goals are those which we set to achieve our real goals. There may be many different paths, or derived goals, which can fulfil our real goals. For example, many people interested in social service keep civil services as their goal. However, joining civil services is a derived goal. The actual goal is to do social service. The derived goal may or may not be achieved, but, the goal of doing social service is more feasible to achieve. That is the main disadvantage of considering our derived goal as the goal. We may or may not be able to achieve a derived goal, as the future is uncertain. It is to be observed that derived goal is just a path to achieve our actual goal where as the real goal can be achieved in many paths. In many cases, the derived goals so replace our real goal that our real goal fades in our brain leaving us with a goal without a reason. A derived goal also blinds our vision of other paths. In case we have diversified interests, we can even satisfy our multiple diversified interests by good planning and right choice.

Intuition is another tool. Learning through intuition is the greatest path of learning. Ask your inner self and listen to it. It gives you all the knowledge and all the power. Learn through it. Know that the essence of life is to achieve what we really love and satisfy your heart. But sadly, many of us are surrendering themselves to the external factors and giving less importance to, and even sometimes forgetting, what our heart needs. Never do this because one day after a few years, you will regret it.

Positive thinking is another tool. It gives us confidence to deal a situation. We can also use this tool to keep us working. For example, if we are pressurised and are thinking if to leave some of our works in which we are actually interested, we can use positive thinking to keep us working. We can strengthen our willingness to work by adding links which will help us to move on. These links include the positive things which we will probably be gaining after completing the task, qualities we will be gaining through the process of doing the task, and self-motivation that you do that to satisfy our heart, and so on.

Negative thinking is an extremely important tool. Confused? Looking both the faces of the coin is important. Seeing both the positives and negatives of a problem or work at your hand is very important. By looking in the positive way, we will develop hope and faith and by looking in the negative way, we will be able to expect the possible consequences and obstacles and will be able to prevent them. And if they are inevitable, we can make ourselves ready to face them. Negative thinking helps in forecasting the possible and negative effects of a situation or the path we are taking. But we have to carefully balance it with positive thinking. An uncontrolled negative thinking is like a forest fire. It destroys everything in its way. For this, we have to understand the purpose of negative thinking. It is just to understand the possible problems ahead. Note that if you doubt your control over the negative thinking, don't use this tool. It just makes us stronger but without a proper control, it can override us.

Music is another tool. Even though, any other thing like some game, dance, subject in which we have interest can be used, I suggest music. The thing we have to do is meditate on it. We have to analyse and understand the inner meaning of music. It gives us great relief, improves our concentration, and if properly used can even provoke our thoughts and motivate us. That is the power of music. For example, when I am not able to concentrate on my work, I listen to music and treat it as a base. By this, if I am not concentrating on the work I am doing, I will switch to music. By this, I am actually preventing my mind from wandering away. So, I can easily come back to the work. Music isn't just some sounds mixed in a way suitable for us to listen. It has immense energy bound in it. Simply meditate over music, it gives you a lot.

The most important feature of a good framework is its stability. Stability means a proper heart-brain relationship. We have to ensure that the system is stable. The external factors and the faulty internal factors together tend to sway our system away from stability. Our system being instable means we are no more in the zone of comfort and happiness. There will always be things pestering you and you will not be in a position to deal with them.

Trying situations, problems and failures can make our system strong or unstable. Their effect of us depends on our attitude towards them. We have to learn to accept situations and challenge them. This removes the fear of problems. We have to understand that problems are inevitable, then why escape them? A problem we solve makes us stronger to face more difficult problems in the future. Problems and failures help us in looking into ourselves and identify our mistakes. Once you start to enjoy problem solving, you don't worry about them. The world is just as we see it, and so is a problem. We feeling it big make it big and we feeling it small make it small. Solving a huge problem makes us tough but solving a problem tactically makes us tougher. Before solving the problem, we have to first understand what the problem really is. We failing here mean we fail to solve the problem. We have to always believe that we are just enough powerful and we can solve the problem. We should neither feel that we are far more powerful than the problem because that creates overconfidence nor feel less powerful as that discourages us. We have to identify our potential. Believe truly that you are powerful, that makes you powerful.

Many times we want to achieve success in solving the problem in the first attempt or in the initial phase of solving it. But we may not achieve it. We needn't be disappointed for that. We should fight back again and with much greater force and better techniques correcting the mistakes we committed previously. We should be happy that we got a strong opponent and can have a lively fight instead of the normal dull ones. This can only be done by taking the problem as a challenge and enjoying the fight. Failure is never an end. It is a lesson for us. It reminds us of our weaknesses and shows our mistakes. The failures can be made stepping stones for success if we learn from them. Thus the ability to learn from our failures is another tool.

14

Understanding Ourselves

Do I Know Me?

"A person starts to live when he can live outside himself."

— Albert Einstein

True wisdom comes to us when we realize how little we understand about life, ourselves and the world around us.

— Frank Herbert

When I was 5 years old, my mother always told me that happiness was the key to life. When I went to school, they asked me what I wanted to be when I grew up. I wrote down 'happy'. They told me I didn't understand the assignment, and I told them they didn't understand life.

— John Lennon

Each of us has a world in us. But do we understand our world? It is a question with an uncertain answer. It is a question we pay negligible importance and yet is very fundamental and important. We have different answers for it. Some yeses and some noes and some silence. Many times, we feel some void in us. We feel confused about ourselves. We feel something is pulling us inside. We hear a voice in us, our own, trying to talk to us, yet we hardly listen to it. The phrases 'inner voice', 'the world in us' are not of spiritual concern or some fantasies seen in books. They are reality.

Don't these signs show there are some parts in you unknown to you? What is the truth? We have to go on a quest for it. The journey is adventurous, risky and of hurdles. Yet the result is more than just worth it. I call it 'adventurous, risky and of hurdles' because we have to face the TRUTH.

When is the last time you thought about yourself? Most people hardly think about themselves. Most of us spend little time and have tiny or no space of mind to spend on themselves. Why is it so? Is it so due to the busy schedule or giving less importance to ourselves or due to some other reason? But aren't we the most important person for us? So let us just take off some time to work on ourselves.

Life is a mess of uncertainty. We encounter many situations and some of them trying. They influence us in many ways. Sometimes they change us eminently. A small scolding from a teacher might disinterest the student from that subject or whole of education. A small scolding from parent on committing a mistake may push the child towards depressive nature or he might learn from the mistake and build up a good character. The pressure due to education or career may cause a teenager to try to escape from everything. These influences of the things happening around us persist through out our life. During the childhood it is due to our sensitivity. During the teenage, it is due to the huge turbulence of things happening around us. Each stage has its own level of importance.

But how good is it to get directly influenced by the things around us? Is it good to make us too pliable to the situations that we lose ourselves? What are we at the end? Is it good to let life control what we are? Can we become what we want and be what we want to be with such a nature? No! We need to preserve ourselves and build ourselves consciously. It is only then that we can be what we want to be.

Understanding ourselves is the fundamental part of it. And we achieve it by thinking it about ourselves. We spend time for our works, our family, our friends, entertainment. And we ought to spend time for ourselves.

Just sit in a quite place and start thinking about yourself. Think not about your works or your friends or something else. Think only about you. What is the first thing that comes to your mind? Nothing! Most of us face a low level of incompetence on thinking about ourselves. We have to raise that level, and it is by thinking. When you start thinking about yourselves, you face void due to which you don't get any thoughts and your mind appears to be blank. And then you get thoughts that you know everything about yourselves. But you have to fight them and continue thinking. These are the tiny hurdles in the path for self-revelation.

Initially, it is tough to think about ourselves. Thoughts like:

What should I think about? What is it that I don't understand about me? Are there really any parts of me that I am unaware of? It is simply time waste for me to think about me. I have too many works to be completed.

But fight with your thoughts and keep moving. The most straight forward method is to question ourselves. Assume that you are some other person. Live outside you and question yourself as another person. It may seem ridiculous, but is a very effective. When we are considering us as some other person, I become you. Questions arise, doubts arise, fact that you don't know about that other person (its you) is evident. Just start revealing yourself to your image. The more you reveal, the better you feel and the better you understand yourself.

If it is difficult to talk to yourself, simply write a letter to you. Write what you think about you, what you are inside, what your likes and dislike, strengths and weaknesses, and interests are, and so on. Remember that you needn't show it to anyone but yourself. Write about none but 'you'. After writing it, just keep it safely. Read it the next day and refine it. Then reply to it. Don't treat this as waste of time but write all of your thoughts and feelings. In fact writing in some ways is better than directly talking to self, and of course the latter is better in some ways. If you want it to be more lively, chat with yourself by texting in phone or writing your questions and replies on pieces of paper. Each method has its own strengths. It is better to use all the methods employing one method at a time at random.

But this still leaves a few doubts in us. What should we think about? Ask yourself. Listen to your inner voice: intuition. You will get it. Preliminarily ask questions like: What are my strengths and weaknesses? Where am I lacking? How do I think? What are the lapses in my thought process? And so on. Ask questions and find answers. Once you start understanding yourself, you will know what you have to think about.

Build You

Each person's world is beautiful in its own way. We have ours and it is beautiful. Do you enjoy it? Did you ever feel that you are beautiful inside? Did you ever embrace yourself? Well no means, you haven't visited your world. This time don't just think, but feel. Just go digging deep into you. See your world. Visualize the world in you. But this can only be achieved by initially thinking about you.

I believe in building ourselves. We are not robots to be programmed by someone or dolls to be played as someone's choice. But we are humans. We have our own individuality. We are our own life-makers, of course with the society playing its role. We have a world in us and we need to preserve it by shielding it from the external influences. We have to understand how each situation influences and pass on the positive ones and remove the negatives. We should not let life and the situations in it decide the way we are. At the same time, we have to follow some universal ethics and have some for ourselves.

Letting yourself sway in the wind of life leads you to lose yourselves. We have to stand on what we are and at the same time accept life as it comes filtering out the unwanted and unethical things. We have to understand ourselves and then build an internal system to monitor and control us. Think about each step you do. Analyse yourself. Feel the beauty of yourself. Identify your strengths and weaknesses. Understand your thought process. Monitor them and make them better by correcting your mistakes and employing better methods. Define meaning for your life and devise your ethics and principles. Follow your dreams.

Whole of this process starts with a single question. Ask yourself the most importance question,

'Do I Know Me?'

15

Live Your Life
Your Way

"It is good to have an end to journey toward; but it is the journey that matters, in the end."

— Ernest Hemingway

"Far away there in the sunshine are my highest aspirations. I may not reach them, but I can look up and see their beauty, believe in them, and try to follow where they lead."

— Louisa May Alcott

"Arise, Awake, Stop not until your goal is achieved."

— Swami Vivekananda

Never leave aims and interests. Whatever may be the circumstances, never leave them! Do you know why? Because that is the essence of your life! I interviewed many people from drivers to students to well-settled people about their aims. Most of them are not happy. Even though they were able to do well in what they are doing, they are not satisfied deep in heart. The reason is, they didn't do what they wanted to. Due to lack of interest at that time or due to external problems or due to ill-influences, they didn't do what they wanted to. There are drivers who stopped their school education in middle due to influence of friends. There are students interested in some other field joining engineering streams due to pressures from family or society with the normal belief that engineering is the major and the only stream where we get good jobs. There are artists who have to suppress their passion for art due to academic pressures. There are employees who earn huge amounts f money doing a job they like.

Is this what we are struggling all our life for? Doing something we don't like and not doing something we have a heart for. Come on! It is our life. We ought to live it our way. I am not asking you to go against your parents or the society. But try to convince them. Tell them what you really want. Tell them the scope you have in that field. Tell about your capabilities. There will be pressures. There will be hurdles. But your life is worth the struggle. If you are not able to convince them, then don't fall back. But struggle further. Take your path on your own, which is less preferred, or take both the paths. Build up a strategy to satisfy your interests and your parents' desires. For example, if you are interested in music and your parents want to take engineering as stream, then, do engineering for them, but with interest, and learn and try for careers in music. Once you have achieved something in field of your interest, all your hurdles will start falling. It is the same even if you have diversified interests. Following one interest doesn't mean leaving other. For example, you have interest in different subjects like mathematics, physics and psychology; try to satisfy all of them. Search for where they converge and go in that path. If they don't converge, follow the path where you satisfy most of your interest and work on other interests independently.

In The Alchemist, Paulo Coelho said,

"And, when you want something, all the universe conspires in helping you to achieve it."

It is true. When you desire and start working on something, the paths around you open up. You will have options bubbling out of dark showing you the path. But it has its struggle to face. You may or may not achieve something exceptional or outstanding. Or you may not even make much progress in the field of your interest. But believe in me, you will be satisfied and happy. The struggle you face fills you with peace. You will fill up the void in you.

Life is a choice to make, whether to work on what you want or on what others want. I choose to have no other choice than working on what I want. Choose yours. Don't fear the hurdles. Come forward and fight the world. Be what you are.

"Take up one idea. Make that one idea your life; dream of it; think of it; live on that idea. Let the brain, the body, muscles, nerves, every part of your body be full of that idea, and just leave every other idea alone. This is the way to success, and this is the way great spiritual giants are produced." Swami Vivekananda

It is when you follow your dreams that you live up to yourself. Base all the work you do to your interests. Keep the material things like the scope, public status, salary, and so on to secondary. Each job has its own importance and value. The value of the job is decided by us. By what we put in it and how much we are interested in it. If we treat engineering or doctor as the best career, do we have great leaders, sportsmen, actors, and managers? You enjoy life when you take it as it comes and be what you want to be.

Be yourself. Live for yourself. That's life!

16

A Word by the Author

"We are what our thoughts have made us; so take care about what you think. Words are secondary. Thoughts live; they travel far."

— Swami Vivekananda

The theories in this book may help you to get a better understanding of you and techniques will be helpful to build a better you. Everything in the world is relative. What works for me may not work for you and what works for you may not work for some other person. The difference is due to the difference in the states of the mind and the heart. So the better way is, don't use these techniques as they are. Understand the inner value and essence of them and then mould them to suit you and more importantly, create your own techniques and theories which suit you using this book. I tried to present the techniques and theories in almost universally adaptable way. Developing your own techniques by understanding the theories is advised. We have to note that we are highly adaptable to everything. So, a technique may not work for us for long time. So, we have to keep changing the techniques. This helps us in maintaining proper balance. After implementing the techniques, monitor the progress continuously.

All the best! May you be what you aspire to be.

17

Quotes

A Source of Inspiration

Words are very powerful. I believe in their power to bring change. They inspire, guide and fill us with astounding energy. They give us as much as we extract. Here are a few quotes by people who inspired the world through her words and actions.

"To love oneself is the beginning of a life-long romance."
— Oscar Wilde

"Enjoy yourself; for there is nothing in the world we can call our own".
— Maltese Proverb

"Life is a song – sing it. Life is a game-play it. Life is a challenge-meet it. Life is a dream-realize it. Life is a sacrifice-offer it. Life is a love-enjoy it."
— Sai Baba

"Know yourself, master yourself; conquest of self is most gratifying. Build life for yourself"

"There are only two ways to live your life. One is as though nothing is a miracle. The other is as though everything is a miracle."
— Albert Einstein

"Sometimes people are beautiful.

Not in looks.

Not in what they say.

Just in what they are."

— Markus Zusak, I am the Messenger

"There is nothing noble in being superior to your fellow man; true nobility is being superior to your former self."

— Ernest Hemingway

"Those who cannot change their minds cannot change anything."

— George Bernard Shaw

"Make the most of yourself....for that is all there is of you."

— Ralph Waldo Emerson

"Learn to enjoy every minute of your life. Be happy now. Don't wait for something outside of yourself to make you happy in the future. Think how really precious is the time you have to spend, whether it's at work or with your family. Every minute should be enjoyed and savored."

— Earl Nightingale

"Life isn't about finding yourself. Life is about creating yourself."

— George Bernard Shaw

"Be who you are and say what you feel because those who mind don't matter and those who matter don't mind."

— Dr. Seuss

"No matter who you are, no matter what you did, no matter where you've come from, you can always change, become a better version of yourself."

— Madonna

"Always dream and shoot higher than you know you can do. Do not bother just to be better than your contemporaries or predecessors. Try to be better than yourself."

— **William Faulkner**

"Once we accept our limits, we go beyond them."

— **Albert Einstein**

"Formal education will make you a living; self-education will make you a fortune."

— **Jim Rohn**

"Do your best, and be a little better than you are."

— **Gordon B. Hinckley**

"The curious paradox is that when I accept myself just as I am, then I can change."

— **Carl R. Rogers**

"It's not what you say out of your mouth that determines your life, it's what you whisper to yourself that has the most power!"

— **Robert T. Kiosaki**

"When you concentrate your energy purposely on the future possibility that you aspire to realize, your energy is passed on to it and makes it attracted to you with a force stronger than the one you directed towards it."

— **Stephen Richards**

Think Your way to Success: Let Your Dreams Run Free

"And, when you want something, all the universe conspires in helping you to achieve it."

— **Paulo Coelho,** *The Alchemist*

"Obstacles are things a person sees when he takes his eyes off his goal."

— **E. Joseph Cossman**

"A goal is not always meant to be reached, it often serves simply as something to aim at."

— **Bruce Lee**

"It's the possibility of having a dream come true that makes life interesting."

— **Paulo Coelho,** *The Alchemist*

"The simple things are also the most extraordinary things, and only the wise can see them."

— **Paulo Coelho,** *The Alchemist*

"Reach high, for stars lie hidden in you. Dream deep, for every dream precedes the goal."

— **Rabindranath Tagore**

Index

A

Aims, 76

Alcott, Louisa May, 76

Ambedkar, B.R., 42

Ancient Greeeks, 2

Anger, 5

B

Blind faith, 6

Bono, Edward de, 64

Brain, 7-8

orderly, 7

stable, 7

Buddha, 54

C

Childhood, 35

Controlling elements, 4

Controlling the mind energy, 42-50

brain, 46

breathing technique, 48

concentration, 47

conceptual schemes, 43

cosmic energy, 43

deviations, 50

establishment, 42

external factors, 49

feeling, 45

minimizing deviation, 48

music, 48

releasing the hidden energy, 46

science, 44

task to identify, 43

version of right, 43

Converting negatives into positives, 51-53

confused, 51

improve positive qualities, 51

reduce negative qualities, 51

Cumulative nature, 9

D

Distorting factors, 5

Dreams, 1

E

Educational psychology, 1

Educational stress, 16

Educational system, 14

Effect of a friend, 34, 45

Einstein, Albert, 12, 20, 51, 60, 63, 71

F

Faith, 23

Fear, 5

Feelings, 5

Framework of mind, 64-70
application of art of differentiation, 67
ethics, 65
goals, 67
integrated system of hearth, 64
intuition, 68
music, 69
negative thinking, 68
order, 65
positive thinking, 68
principles, 65
rules and limits, 65
stability, 69
systematic, 66
tools and techniques, 67
Friends and society, 34-37
graduation level, 36
higher school education, 36
pre-school days, 35
primary school days, 35
senior secondary education, 36
state after studies, 37
Friendship, 34, 37
Frustration, 5

G

Greville, 54

H

Hard work, 20
Heart, 5-7
Hemingway, Ernest, 76
Herbert, Frank, 71
Hindrance, 9

I

Ideal education system, 60-63
main advantage, 61
students; brain, 61
troubling factors, 61
Ideal students, 57-59, 60
attitude, 58
environment, 59
future vision, 59
ideal machine, 57
mean, 57
qualities, 58
target, 59
Imagination, 21
Important qualities, 19
Instantaneous state, 11
Interests, 76

J

Judgement of a person, 10

K

Kall, 4, 54
Kennedy, John, 57
King, Martin Luthar, 60
Knowledge, 21

L

Lama, Dalai, 4
Lennon, John, 71
Life is a mess of uncertainty, 72
Live your life, 76-78
Logical thinking, 38-41
application of logic, 40
developing the thought, 41
how to develop logical thinking, 39
knowledge, 39

logic maps, 40
technique of retracing the thoughts, 39
understand logic, 41
very essence of education, 38-39

M

Mental framework, 2
Mental structure, 1
Milton, John, 38

N

Negative effects, 18
Negative thinking, 9
New educational system, 63

O

Origin of stress, 16

P

Parents, 26-33
advise, 32
analyse them, 30
balance between the outer word and the environment, 31
bound limits, 28
effect of society, 29
first teachers, 26
importance, 26
negative attitude of child, 29
observe the child, 31
parents' judgements, 31
parents' role, 33
prime factors, 29
reliving the childhood, 30
role of parents, 26
synchronization, 27
Passion, 59
Path of logic, 5
Patton, Gen. George, 60
Positive part of stress, 18
Psychology, 1
Pure faith, 6

Q

Quotes, 80-83

R

Radiating energy, 20
Relationship, 8
Repulsion towards friendship, 35
Robbins, Anthony, 64
Role of education, 14
Role of friendship, 35
Roosevelt, Franklin D., 6

S

Self-analysis, 54-56
external factors, 55
non-retreating efforts, 56
understand the character and actions, 55
ways to self-analysis, 55
Self-confidence, 23
Sensitive elements, 8
Sensitivity, 7
Shakespeare, William, 34
Strength, 21
Stress 13
Students and education system, 12-18
effect of education on thinking, 14-15
effect of education system on students' behavior, 15-18

- present educational system, 12-14
- stress, 13

Students' strengths, 19-25
- effect of faith on us, 24
- faith in us, 23
- scope, 24-25

Synchronization, 27

T

Thinking, 15

Truth, 72

Twain, Mark, 12

U

Understand ourselves, 71
- build you, 74
- thoughts, 73-74

V

Virtual limits, 25

Vivekananda (Swami), 19, 47, 77, 79

W

Worst properties, 9

Y

Youth, 42

Z

Zeal, 58, 59